NEW DIRECTIONS FOR TEACHING AND LEARNING

Robert J. Menges, *Northwestern University*
EDITOR-IN-CHIEF

Marilla D. Svinicki, *University of Texas, Austin*
ASSOCIATE EDITOR

Collaborative Learning: Underlying Processes and Effective Techniques

Kris Bosworth
Indiana University

Sharon J. Hamilton
Indiana University, Indianapolis

EDITORS

Number 59, Fall 1994

JOSSEY-BASS PUBLISHERS
San Francisco

COLLABORATIVE LEARNING: UNDERLYING PROCESSES
AND EFFECTIVE TECHNIQUES
Kris Bosworth, Sharon J. Hamilton (eds.)
New Directions for Teaching and Learning, no. 59
Robert J. Menges, Editor-in-Chief
Marilla D. Svinicki, Associate Editor

Microfilm copies of issues and articles are available in 16mm and 35mm,
as well as microfiche in 105mm, through University Microfilms Inc., 300
North Zeeb Road, Ann Arbor, Michigan 48106-1346.

LC 85-644763   ISSN 0271-0633   ISBN 0-7879-9998-9

NEW DIRECTIONS FOR TEACHING AND LEARNING is part of The Jossey-Bass
Higher and Adult Education Series and is published quarterly by Jossey-
Bass Inc., Publishers, 350 Sansome Street, San Francisco, California
94104-1342. Second-class postage paid at San Francisco, California, and
at additional mailing offices. POSTMASTER: Send address changes to New
Directions for Teaching and Learning, Jossey-Bass Inc., Publishers, 350
Sansome Street, San Francisco, California 94104-1342.

SUBSCRIPTIONS for 1994 cost $47.00 for individuals and $62.00 for institutions, agencies, and libraries.

EDITORIAL CORRESPONDENCE should be sent to the editor-in-chief, Robert J.
Menges, Northwestern University, Center for the Teaching Professions,
2003 Sheridan Road, Evanston, Illinois 60208-2610.

Cover photograph by Richard Blair/Color & Light © 1990.

CONTENTS

About This Publication. Since 1980, *New Directions for Teaching and Learning (NDTL)* has brought a unique blend of theory, research, and practice to leaders in postsecondary education. *NDTL* sourcebooks strive not only for solid substance but also for timeliness, compactness, and accessibility.

The series has four goals: to inform readers about current and future directions in teaching and learning in postsecondary education, to illuminate the context that shapes these new directions, to illustrate these new directions through examples from real settings, and to propose ways in which these new directions can be incorporated into still other settings.

This publication reflects our view that teaching deserves respect as a high form of scholarship. We believe that significant scholarship is conducted not only by researchers who report results of empirical investigations but also by practitioners who share disciplined reflections about teaching. Contributors to *NDTL* approach questions of teaching and learning as seriously as they approach substantive questions in their own disciplines, and they deal not only with pedagogical issues but also with the intellectual and social context in which these issues arise. Authors deal on the one hand with theory and research and on the other with practice, and they translate from research and theory to practice and back again.

About This Volume. So that readers can explore why the method of collaborative learning works the way it does, Kris Bosworth and Sharon J. Hamilton asked contributors to this volume to discuss the processes underlying the collaborative learning paradigm. Those contributors examine the theories of collaborative learning, ranging from group process to individual development. The resulting volume, which is intended for practitioners who have taken the first steps, stands as a nice counterpoint to other published works on the basic pragmatics of collaborative learning.

Robert J. Menges, *Editor-in-Chief*
Marilla D. Svinicki, *Associate Editor*

ROBERT J. MENGES, editor-in-chief, is professor of education and social policy at Northwestern University and senior researcher, National Center on Post-secondary Teaching, Learning, and Assessment.

MARILLA D. SVINICKI, associate editor, is director of the Center for Teaching Effectiveness, University of Texas at Austin.

EDITORS' NOTES

We learn collaboratively from the day we are born. Language, paralinguistic behavior, and the games and chores of life are all learned in social interaction. In its institutionalized forms, social interaction has long been a part of traditional college education, particularly in medicine and the lab sciences. Nevertheless, higher education has relied on the information-transmitting lecture. Now, however, changing demographics, the information explosion, and increasingly well-articulated theories of optimal learning conditions are transforming how we look at teaching in our colleges and universities. Collaborative learning is increasingly acknowledged as an effective way of engaging students with discipline-specific language and concepts, acquainting them with the social responsibilities of learning and the intellectual benefits of shared explorations for meaning, and retaining them by improving their performance and enjoyment of learning.

Indeed, the process of creating this volume exemplifies the benefits of collaboration. We each had a very particular notion of collaborative learning. Kris had an eclectic acceptance of the principles of both cooperative learning and collaborative learning. In contrast, Sharon favored the epistemological assumptions of collaborative learning and viewed the strategies prescribed for cooperative learning with some skepticism. In the process of sorting through the more than thirty case studies that we received in response to a request published in *The Chronicle of Higher Education,* we each came to understand the values inherent in the other's stance. Our conversations primed Sharon to take advantage of models of collaborative learning that John Trimbur was developing and sparked the developmental model for the establishment of collaborative learning classrooms that she describes in Chapter Nine. And working with Sharon helped Kris to move away from a pragmatic "just do it" approach and develop a more thoughtful theory-based focus. Instead of distinction, there is now congruence between what she believes about learning and what she does in her classroom.

This volume explores the underlying processes of and current effective practices in collaborative learning. The exploration balances history and theory with specific, practical suggestions. In Chapter One, Jeanne Marcum Gerlach questions what collaboration is and how it manifests itself in higher education and offers some practical suggestions about managing collaborative learning in the classroom. In Chapter Two, James Flannery looks at the role of knowledge in the collaborative learning classroom and discusses the differing epistemological imperatives of lecture-transmission, cooperative learning, and collaborative learning. Recognizing that well begun is half done, Kris Bosworth writes in Chapter Three of the need to develop students' explicit awareness of the social skills that they must possess if effective collaborative learning is to occur. She delineates several categories of social skills. Some are essential prerequisites. All develop throughout the collaborative process, particularly when we make students aware of their importance. Building on the social skills of particular learners in Chapter Four, Judith Miller, John Trimbur, and John Wilkes present a case study of a biology class that shows how different personality styles influence the nature of learning in a collaborative environment.

Thinking, speaking, and learning are so interdependent that we can virtually assume a correlative relationship between collaborative learning and critical thinking. In Chapter Five, Craig Nelson meticulously delineates the interrelationship in both theoretical and practical terms. It is essential today to consider how technology can be used to enhance student learning. In Chapter Six, Patricia Sullivan uses writing instruction to illustrate how collaborative learning can be integrated with technology. Learning, thinking, and writing all have to be assessed regularly in the classroom, formally and informally, formatively and summatively. Collaborative processes and the products of collaboration pose special problems. In Chapter Seven, Sharon Cramer discusses various assessment needs and describes several assessment tools and strategies, including tools and strategies for the assessment of collaborative processes and products. Chapter Eight presents three case studies that we selected from those received in response to the request that we placed in *The Chronicle of Higher Education*. Allen Emerson (mathematics), Jerry Phillips (literacy), and Cathy Hunt and Arlene Bowman Alexander (anatomy and physiology) describe the activities in their collaborative classrooms and their reasons for using collaboration. In Chapter Nine, an overview of the various models of collaborative learning, Sharon Hamilton outlines the process by which one develops expertise in the establishment of collaborative learning classrooms and describes a model that supports the efforts of faculty working with collaborative learning at various stages of comfort and competence.

Collaborative learning may well be the most significant pedagogical shift of the century for teaching and learning in higher education. It has the potential to transform learners' and instructors' views of learning, knowing, and understanding as it acquaints students with the skills needed to cooperate, negotiate, and formulate productive responses to the changing demands of this increasingly complex world. We believe that this volume provides significant guidance in helping this shift to occur.

This volume is the result of years of collaborative effort with colleagues, mentors, and students. Kris thanks her once and future collaborators David H. Gustafson, Robert Hawkins, Phyllis Gingiss, Thomas Welsh, Gerald Smith, Robert Harris, Trudy Karlson, William Hanson, and Ann Schaffer. Sharon thanks William Plater and Erv Boschmann for their support of the Indiana University Inter-Campus Group on Collaborative Learning; her colleagues in the English department who have enabled her to explore aspects of collaborative learning; and her mentors, James Britton, Harold Rosen, and

John Dixon, who introduced her to the social nature of learning. Both authors thank Dana Greene Little for organizational and editorial contributions and support.

Kris Bosworth
Sharon J. Hamilton
Editors

KRIS BOSWORTH *is assistant professor in curriculum and instruction and director of the Center for Adolescent Studies at Indiana University. Her research interests are in the development of educational programs that promote positive and healthy social, emotional, and cognitive development.*

SHARON J. HAMILTON *is associate professor of English in the School of Liberal Arts, Indiana University at Indianapolis, author of* My Name's Not Susie, *and coeditor of* Sourcebook for Collaborative Learning in the Arts and Sciences.

This chapter discusses the characteristics that successful collaborative learning situations share and offers suggestions for incorporating these characteristics into content area courses.

Is This Collaboration?

Jeanne Marcum Gerlach

> I always enjoy returning to perform on "Saturday Night Live,"
> because it's the only time I can engage in true collaboration.
> —Bill Murray, Feb. 20, 1993

When I heard Bill Murray, the film and television comedian, make the comment just quoted, I wondered exactly what he meant, and I thought of my own collaborative efforts both in and out of the classroom. I also thought about my attempts to write this chapter—how, in many ways, the effort has been such a lonely, individual experience, which seems ironic in that the chapter is about collaboration. The thoughts soon passed, and I forgot about Murray's comment until one of my students reminded me of it.

"Hey, Doctor Gerlach, did you hear what Bill Murray said about collaboration on 'Saturday Night Live' last week?" Not giving me time to answer, the student continued, "Is that what we're doing in this class? You know, collaboration—the kind of collaboration they do on 'Saturday Night Live'?"

"Well, yes, you might say we are doing something very similar to what the actors on 'Saturday Night Live' do in regard to collaboration. For example . . ."

As I began to respond to the student's question, the other students reminded me that the period was over. Students from another class were waiting impatiently at the door. I realized that I would have to wait a week to answer the student's question. To help the entire class continue to think about how collaboration works both inside and outside the classroom, I asked the students to think about Murray's comment, to think about what they know about collaboration, and to respond in their journals to their fellow student's question, "Does collaboration in this class work the same way it does on 'Saturday Night Live'?"

New Directions for Teaching and Learning, no. 59, Fall 1994 © Jossey-Bass Publishers

Since the class met only once each week, I had some time to think about how I was going to answer the student's question. While trying to formulate a definitive answer, I began to think about writing this chapter, a chapter in which I had intended to offer conclusive guidelines to college professors about how collaboration works and about how collaborative activities can be used effectively in classrooms. Although the audiences to whom I am responding are different—one consists of my students, the other of my colleagues—I hesitate to offer precise answers or guidelines to either group. Let me explain my indecisiveness.

When Sharon Hamilton and Kris Bosworth invited me to write a nuts-and-bolts chapter for this *New Directions* sourcebook, I was pleased to accept. I know that the concept of collaborative learning is becoming increasingly visible in American higher education. Following the lead of teachers and researchers (Bruffee, 1973, 1978, 1982, 1984, 1985; Elbow, 1973, 1981; Gere, 1987), a number of college and university professors are initiating and developing courses that emphasize collaborative learning across the curriculum. Part of this initiative is a result of recommendations from scholars and researchers that faculty at all levels of higher education become familiar with and involved in the promotion of collaborative learning at their institutions.

Further, because collaborative learning has been shown to be more successful in promoting achievement than either individualized or competitive learning experiences (Johnson and others, 1981), it seemed to me that it should be both the concern of and attractive to all educators. Yet the attitudes about collaborative learning that I encountered among my colleagues were predominantly negative. Many faculty members do not see collaborative learning as important in their courses. Some feel that it is just another fad: here today, gone tomorrow. Many arts and science faculty feel that the responsibility for teaching about collaborative learning belongs solely to education faculty. They argue that they have enough to do just to cover the content of their courses. Many believe that an effort to incorporate collaborative learning activities into their teaching would increase their already heavy work loads. Some honestly admit that they have no idea of what collaborative learning is or should be. They often lack either the confidence or the knowledge needed to experiment with collaborative learning activities in their classrooms.

For all these reasons, I felt that I needed to write a chapter that explained what college and university faculty need to know about collaborative learning in order to use it in their classrooms to enhance content learning for their students. Because I knew that other chapters of the book would give readers the historical and theoretical framework that justifies the value of collaborative learning, I initially intended to tell my audience of colleagues how to incorporate collaborative learning into classroom activities so that students could work productively in groups to learn course content, connect it with knowledge that they had acquired in the past, and synthesize them in order to make new knowledge. However, as I worked on the chapter, I began to realize that I could not provide readers with fail-safe guidelines for the tasks that I had set for myself.

At this point, I must pause to tell readers that my interest in collaborative learning grows out of my own positive experiences with it. During the past ten years, I have asked college and university students in various courses at the undergraduate, master's, and doctoral levels to work in collaborative groups. Many of the collaborations were designed by instinct. Many were tasks previously intended for individual completion but adapted for group use. Although it is still not entirely clear to me what these collaborations did for my students, I am pleased enough with the interest in content material that they generated to use them regularly in my courses. I still do not really know what one learns about course content through collaboration. While many professors report that collaboration has a positive influence, few can say exactly what collaboration contributes. The studies on why, how, or even whether collaboration actually affects students' attitudes, class participation, or content learning are relatively few, and most of the research on collaborative learning has been conducted at the K–12 level (Johnson, Maruyama, Johnson, Nelson, and Skon, 1981; Slavin, 1983). These researchers conducted meta-analyses on the effect of collaborative learning on academic achievement. They found that achievement gains for students involved in collaborative learning were larger than gains for students using more traditional, individual learning approaches. As already noted, while relatively few studies have been conducted on collaborative learning at the college level, research has found significant achievement effects (Dansereau, 1983; Frierson, 1986; Triesman, 1986).

In addition to my own classroom experiences with collaboration, I continue to explore the historical and theoretical basis (Barnes, Britton, and Rosen, 1971; Britton, 1972; Bruffee, 1973, 1978, 1982, 1984, 1985, 1986, 1988; Elbow, 1973, 1981; Elbow and Belanoff, 1989; Gere, 1987; LeFevre, 1987; Lunsford and Ede, 1986, 1990; Rorty, 1983; Trimbur, 1989; Vygotsky, 1962) for collaborative learning that informs my classroom practice. Rereading Lunsford and Ede (1990), I realized that they had faced a dilemma similar to mine. They, too, had envisioned developing specific guidelines about collaborative activities that teachers could use in the classroom. They soon realized that it would be difficult to develop specific guidelines because "to proffer definitive guidelines and suggestions to teachers reflects the capacity of collaborative writing to 'open out' or problematize both the theory and practice" (Lunsford and Ede, 1990, p. 122). The authors just cited are talking about collaborative activities in the context of collaborative writing. I believe that the same holds true for other kinds of collaborations. I also agree with Lunsford and Ede (1990) that we cannot assume that activities that prepare students to work successfully in one collaborative setting will empower them to function successfully in other collaborative environments. Lunsford and Ede (1990) resolve their dilemma by abandoning the idea of formulating specific and detailed guidelines and instead writing a chapter suggesting that there are other important concerns about collaborations that need to be addressed. They ask how race, class, and gender issues affect collaboration in the classroom and the workplace. They state that "at present, [they] have only the vaguest of answers" to these questions (Lunsford and Ede, 1990, p. 122).

How relieved I was to learn that I was not alone in believing that there are no definite guidelines for addressing the characteristics of effective collabora-tive learning assignments, especially in regard to organizing and evaluating col-laborative groups. If I think back now on conversations with colleagues, I realized that many admitted to having experienced both successful and unsuc-cessful collaborations in their courses. So, while educators seem to agree that successful collaborative learning activities vary substantially in goals, methods, and desired outcomes, most substantial collaborative learning situations share similar characteristics. This chapter discusses some of those characteristics and offers suggestions for incorporating them into content area courses.

What Is Collaborative Learning?

Collaborative learning is based on the idea that learning is a naturally social act in which the participants talk among themselves. It is through the talk that learning occurs. Britton (Britton and others, 1975) discusses the relationship between talk and writing in the learning process. "Talk is more expressive— the speaker is not obliged to keep himself in the background as he may be in writing; talk relies on an immediate link with listeners, usually a group or whole class; the rapid exchanges of conversation allow many things to go on at once—exploration, clarification, shared interpretation, insight into differ-ences of opinion, illustration and anecdote, explanation by gesture, expression of doubt; and if something is not clear, you can go on until it is" (Britton, 1972, p. 29).

We know that we learn from sharing our ideas, beliefs, and writing through our interactions with others. For example, I have shared this manu-script at different stages of its development with two colleagues. The sharing, a form of collaboration, made the somewhat individual process that I spoke of at the beginning of this chapter more meaningful, more exciting. Regardless of the topic that I am writing about, I know that talking about it with colleagues helps me to clarify information and organize it in a way that makes it clear both to me and to my readers. Vygotsky (1962) argues that learners need to be active organizers who use language in continual interaction with the social world in order to change both the world and themselves. He believes that social interchange is essential to human development and that, as learners use language to communicate with others, their speech expresses their growing awareness and understanding of the topic being discussed and thus interacts with cognitive development. Smith and MacGregor (1992) build on these views when they remind us that the idea of collaborative learning is based on several premises: First, learning is an active, constructive process in which students integrate new material with prior knowledge to create new ideas and new meaning. Second, learning depends on rich contexts that ask students to collaborate with peers to identify and solve problems by engaging in higher-order reasoning and problem-solving skills. Third, learners are diverse and have different backgrounds and experiences. The various perspectives that emerge during collaborative work clarify and illuminate learning for all involved—the student, the members of the collaborative group, and the teacher. Fourth, learning is a social act in which students talk to learn. This social interaction often improves the participants' understanding of the topic under consideration. Fifth, learning has affective and subjective dimensions. Collaborative activities are both socially and emotionally demanding and most often require students not only to articulate their own points of view but also to listen to the views of others. Students realize that they can work with others to create knowledge and meaning. They no longer have to rely solely on the teacher and the textbook.

In light of the premises just reviewed, professors might decide to increase the emphasis placed on the social development of the intellect and decrease the focus on individual intellectual development. They might draw on recent theory and experimental research supporting the idea that, if institutions of higher education are to provide for the optimum intellectual development of students, professors must take collaborative learning seriously across the curriculum.

Many educators have not emphasized collaborative learning in their classrooms. They have rejected the idea in favor of traditional individualized instruction. When one thinks of traditional schools, one often pictures classrooms in which students sit one behind the other at brown wooden or metal desks arranged in straight rows. The professor, always at the front of the classroom, lectures from a text or an outline on a given subject, such as history, math, science, or social studies. The students take notes—copies of the professor's words—and memorize them for later recitation or testing. The main emphasis in such classrooms seems always to be on quietness and order, as if learning occurred only when silence prevailed. Students seldom have an opportunity to exchange thoughts and ideas. They speak only when the teacher asks them to do so—to answer a question or read a written report about a topic that the teacher has assigned. The image of Dickens's Gradgrind school which emphasized facts, facts, facts, comes to mind. In the traditional classroom, the emphasis is almost always on individual learning; students work alone and often compete with one another for class standing.

While there are times when a student wants to investigate a topic of interest, read a novel, or write an essay on his or her own, there are other times when the same student needs to work collaboratively with peers to reach a clearer understanding of the topic being discussed. Even though some research indicates that collaborative learning environments have many advantages for students' intellectual and social development over traditional classrooms that emphasize individualized learning, collaborative learning opportunities in many higher education classrooms are still uncommon.

Scholarship suggests that collaborative learning has many benefits. As noted earlier, research (Johnson and Johnson, 1983; Slavin, 1983) indicates that social interaction leads to advanced cognitive development and promotes higher academic achievement than individualistic learning activities do. If we take this research seriously, then we must reject the idea that learning occurs only in silent classrooms. Rather, learning is enhanced in informal settings where students can move around freely and discuss their thoughts and ideas with peers. Listening to different points of view about how to solve problems or to different perspectives on issues helps students to reach deeper levels of understanding about their subjects. As I noted earlier, there is no single, right way of using collaborative learning. Smith and MacGregor (1992) view *collaborative learning* as an umbrella term that encompasses multiple educational strategies and approaches involving both the teacher and the students in a joint intellectual effort. The methods used usually include having students work in groups of two or more to explore an idea, solve a problem, or create a product. The most important thing to remember is that, while collaborative learning activities vary widely, they all center on the students' processes of investigation, discovery, and application, not on the teacher's presentation of the material (Smith and MacGregor, 1992).

The Role of the Instructor

For the reasons outlined in the preceding section, the main problem for teachers in collaborative learning is to group students so that they can teach themselves and their peers. There is less direct teaching in a collaborative learning class than there is in the traditional classroom. The teacher becomes a task setter, a classroom manager, and a synthesizer (Bruffee, 1982, 1984, 1985; Weiner, 1986). Teaching becomes a process of creating conditions in which collaborative learning can occur: "What is essential is that the task lead to an answer or solution that can represent as nearly as possible the collective judgment and labor of the group as a whole" (Bruffee, 1985, p. 24). According to Weiner (1986), the teacher's role as task setter encompasses more than developing and assigning the tasks. Rather, the teacher often needs to help students decide how to attack the tasks. For instance, if a history teacher assigns a group of students the task of determining the causes and effects of the Civil War, the history teacher might want to explain to the class how cause-and-effect relationships are determined, how they are related, and how they work.

The teacher aids the collaboration process by assuming managerial duties: helping students to adhere to the time limits that have been set for the completion of individual tasks; seeing that the individual members of each group are fulfilling their roles as recorder, reporter, and synthesizer; and organizing classroom space so that chairs and tables can be grouped efficiently and effectively. Finally, the teacher must help the whole class to analyze and synthesize the information that each group reports at the end of the collaborative session. Thus, by acting in these ways—as task setter, manager, and synthesizer—the teacher engages in a process of creating conditions in which collaborative learning can occur. However, MacGregor (1992) points out that, while collaborative learning communities are worthwhile, it is not unusual to encounter difficulties with group work. She notes that students have been conditioned since high school to function in classrooms where the teacher transmits the information, students do their own work, and questions have only one right answer. Thus, as students move into collaborative learning environments, they must make major shifts in their beliefs about classroom learning behavior. MacGregor (1992) identifies seven shifts that have to take place: from listener, observer, and note taker to active problem solver, contributor, and discussant; from low or moderate expectations of preparation for class to high ones; from a private presence in the classroom with few or no risks to a public one with many risks; from attendance dictated by personal choice to attendance dictated by community expectation; from competition with peers to collaborative work with them; from responsibilities and self-definition associated with learning independently to responsibilities and self-direction associated with learning interdependently; from the notion that teachers and texts are the sole sources of authority and knowledge to the notion that peers, oneself, and the thinking of one's community are additional and important sources of authority and knowledge.

MacGregor (1992) believes that, to accommodate these shifts, faculty members need to set the context and forms for collaborative work so that students can overcome their skepticism and discover the positive aspects of learning through collaboration.

An Example

With this introduction to collaborative learning in mind, the reader may now consider the following illustration: Thirty students in an Introduction to Women's Studies class have been divided into six heterogeneous groups of five. Each group is mixed in gender, race, and ethnic origin. All the students in the class have read the chapter in the text on women and health as well as two articles on the issue, and all have watched a week-long series on women's health on the "Good Morning America" television program. The students' task is to determine whether women's health care needs to become a separate medical specialty. This is a real and timely question, because it is currently being considered and discussed by leaders in the medical profession at the National Institutes of Health and in the American Medical Association. Before the groups answer the question, the teacher helps them decide how to answer the question. For example, the teacher suggests that each group consider defining what is meant by the words *women's health care*. Other issues that groups might want to consider include research on women's health, the need for an academic discipline on women's health, and psychology as it relates to women.

The groups now begin their work. Rather than working individually or only with the teacher, the members of the groups become a collective. Some individuals merge less into the group than others, but each group transcends its individual members and takes on a life of its own. While individual group members may disagree about whether women's health care should become a separate specialty, they know that the group must reach a consensus and that negotiation may thus be needed. The cultural context—the ways in which men and women and the members of various minorities and ethnic groups are socialized into holding different but valid ideas—is what makes the group work.

When a group reaches a consensus, its members help the recorder to decide exactly what information should be reported. The recorders report the information to the other groups, and all groups work toward consensus. Next, the class hears the teacher's perspective. Teacher and class negotiate an answer to the question. Finally, teacher and students evaluate their collaborative process. Was it effective or ineffective? In this way, according to Stranger (1987), students and teacher work together to create knowledge. "Knowledge," she asserts, "in this context, is not being defined as 'fact' handed down by an authority figure; instead, it is something fluid that the group and the teacher create during their interaction" (Stranger, 1987, p. 34). The students and the teacher work to empower one another and create an alternative to the traditional classroom structure.

Characteristics of Collaborative Learning Activities

The kind of collaborative learning assignment just described might be adapted by teachers in all content areas who wish to enhance students' content learning by helping them to engage in successful collaborative learning activities. While assignments can vary in goals, methods, and desired outcomes, most share the following six characteristics: First, they allow time for group consensus to occur. Second, they ask students to complete specific tasks within a given amount of time. Third, they allow the members of groups to negotiate individual roles. Fourth, they encourage group consensus but teach respect for individual diversity and minority views. Fifth, they allow students and teacher to collaborate once group consensus has been reached. Sixth, they ask both students and teacher to evaluate the collaborative process as having been effective or ineffective.

Conclusion

This chapter is no more than an introduction to what can happen in a collaborative classroom. There are many ways of structuring groups to develop collaborative learning assignments and of evaluating the effectiveness of such work. For example, Bosworth describes some strategies for social skills development in Chapter Three. Chapter Six focuses on the evaluation of student performance in collaborative settings. Finally, Chapter Eight presents three case studies. Hamilton and Hansen (1992) and Goodsell and others (1992) offer other case studies. This sourcebook as a whole aims to provide faculty members with a place to start learning about the theoretical premises of collaborative learning as well as about strategies that can be used to include collaborative learning in their instruction. As noted earlier, I had intended originally to give readers conclusive guidelines about incorporating collaborative learning effectively into other classroom activities. However, the writing of this chapter, together with several colleagues, helped me to discover that Jean Mac-Gregor (1992, p. 39) is right: "The richest guides for teachers are their own experiments with teaching, the advice and experience of colleagues, and most importantly, formal and informal feedback from the students themselves. Indeed, the collaborative classroom, brimming with data about the content and quality of student learning, is an ongoing lab for 'classroom research.' The public learning taking place provides immediate feedback for the discerning teacher to use in improving collaborative designs. For faculty who offer the same courses year after year, trying group work is a sure hedge against staleness, in that each refinement of a collaborative learning design and each new class's experience with it recreates [sic] the course in fresh and provocative ways."

Let us now return to my student's question: Is the kind of collaboration that we do in class the kind of collaboration that they do on "Saturday Night Live"? As you can imagine, when my class meets this week, I will ask the students to work collaboratively to answer the question. How do you think they will respond?

References

Barnes, D., Britton, J., and Rosen, H. *Language, the Learner, and the School.* (2nd ed.) Harmondsworth, England: Penguin, 1971.

Britton, J. *Language and Learning.* Harmondsworth, England: Penguin, 1972.

Britton, J., Burgess, T., Martin, N., McLeod, A., and Rosen, H. *The Development of Writing Abilities: 11–18.* London: Macmillan Educational, 1975.

Bruffee, K. "Collaborative Learning: Some Practical Models." *College English,* 1973, *34* (5), 579–586.

Bruffee, K. "The Brooklyn Plan: Attaining Intellectual Growth Through Peer Group Tutoring." *Liberal Education,* 1978, *64* (4), 447–468.

Bruffee, K. "Liberal Education and the Social Justification of Belief." *Liberal Education,* 1982, *68* (2), 95–114.

Bruffee, K. "Peer Tutoring and the 'Conversation of Mankind.'" *College English,* 1984, *46* (7), 635–652.

Bruffee, K. *A Short Course in Writing.* (3rd ed.) Boston: Little, Brown, 1985.

Bruffee, K. "Social Construction, Language, and the Authority of Knowledge: A Bibliographical Essay." *College English,* 1986, *48* (8), 773–790.

Bruffee, K. "On Not Listening in Order to Hear: Collaborative Learning and the Rewards of Classroom Research." *Journal of Basic Writing,* 1988, 7 (1), 3–12.

Dansereau, D. F. *Cooperative Learning: Impact on Acquisition of Knowledge and Skills.* Report No. 341. Abilene, Texas: U.S. Army Research for the Behavioral and Social Sciences, 1983. (ED 243088)

Elbow, P. *Writing Without Teachers.* London: Oxford University Press, 1973.

Elbow, P. *Writing with Power.* London: Oxford University Press, 1981.

Elbow, P., and Belanoff, P. *Sharing and Responding.* New York: Random House, 1989.

Frierson, H. "Two Intervention Methods: Effects on Groups of Predominantly Black Nursing Students' Board Scores." *Journal of Research and Development in Education,* 1986, 19, 18–23.

Gere, A. *Writing Groups: History, Theory, and Implications.* Carbondale: Southern Illinois University Press, 1987.

Goodsell, A., Maher, M., Tinton, V., Smith, B., and MacGregor, J. *Collaborative Learning: A Sourcebook for Higher Education.* University Park, Pa.: National Center on Postsecondary Teaching, Learning, and Assessment, 1992.

Hamilton, S., and Hansen, E. (eds.). *Sourcebook for Collaborative Learning in the Arts and Sciences at Indiana University.* Bloomington: Indiana University, 1992.

Johnson, D. W., and Johnson, R. T. "The Socialization and Achievement Crisis—Are Cooperative Learning Experiences the Solution?" In L. Bickman (ed.), *Applied Social Psychology Annual 4.* Newbury Park, Calif.: Sage, 1983.

Johnson, D. W., Maruyama, G., Johnson, R. T., Nelson, D., and Skon, L. "Effects of Cooperative, Competitive and Individualistic Goal Structures on Achievement: A Meta-analysis." *Psychological Bulletin,* 1981, 89, 47–62.

LeFevre, K. *Invention as a Social Act.* Carbondale: Southern Illinois University Press, 1987.

Lunsford, A., and Ede, L. "Let Them Write—Together." *English Quarterly,* 1986, 18 (4), 119–127.

Lunsford, A., and Ede, L. *Singular Texts/Plural Authors.* Carbondale: Southern Illinois University Press, 1990.

MacGregor, J. "Collaborative Learning: Reframing the Classroom." In A. Goodsell and others (eds.), *Collaborative Learning: A Sourcebook for Higher Education.* University Park, Pa.: National Center on Postsecondary Teaching and Learning Assessment, 1992.

Rorty, R. *Philosophy and the Mirror of Nature.* Princeton, N.J.: Princeton University Press, 1983.

Slavin, R. E. "When Does Cooperative Learning Increase Student Achievement?" *Psychological Bulletin,* 1983, 94, 429–445.

Smith, B., and MacGregor, J. "What Is Collaborative Learning?" In A. Goodsell and others (eds.), *Collaborative Learning: A Sourcebook for Higher Education.* University Park, Pa.: National Center on Postsecondary Teaching and Learning Assessment, 1992.

Stranger, C. A. "The Sexual Politics of the One-to-One Tutorial Approach and Collaborative Learning." In *Teaching Writing Pedagogy, Gender and Equity.* State University of New York Press, 1987.

Trimbur, J. "Consensus and Difference in Collaborative Learning." *College English,* 1989, 51 (6), 602–616.

Triesman, U. "A Study of the Mathematics Performance of Black Students at the University of California, Berkeley" (Doctoral dissertation, University of California, Berkeley). *Dissertation Abstracts International,* 1986, 47, 1641A.

Vygotsky, L. *Thought and Language.* Cambridge, Mass.: MIT Press, 1962.

Wiener, H. "Collaborative Learning in the Classroom: A Guide to Evaluation." *College English,* 1986, 48 (1), 52–61.

JEANNE MARCUM GERLACH is associate professor of English education at West Virginia University.

This chapter argues that all classroom experiences are informed by issues of knowledge and authority and asks whether knowledge is discovered, transmitted, and transcended or whether it is constructed and temporal.

Teacher as Co-conspirator: Knowledge and Authority in Collaborative Learning

James L. Flannery

> The issue at stake is not one of relevance but empowerment. We are not concerned with simply motivating students to learn but rather establishing conditions of learning that enable them to locate themselves in history and to interrogate the adequacy of that location.
> —Henry Giroux and R. I. Simon (1989, p. 3)

The minute hand slowly moves into position. The milling about, chattering, desk moving, and shuffling subside. The instructor, with copies of the syllabus, the texts, and first assignment, assumes the typical position in front of the class and begins, again, to teach the course. The instructor talks to the class, assigns the readings and occasional writing tasks, and leads the class for most if not all the time that they spend together. Some of the students attend to the instructor, some take notes, some stare out the window, and some close their eyes. The structure of a typical college course is familiar to us all.

There have been attempts to alter these familiar structures, to effect a shift in the locus of control and responsibility in the classroom away from the instructor and toward the student. Instructors, although implicated in the very power structures that such shifts challenge, have encouraged these attempts. Student group learning takes the dynamics of classroom life into account, at least in some of its forms. In the public schools, the serious use of small-group learning environments is not new. Examples can be found as long ago the Great Depression, when many schools began to incorporate extracurricular activities into the standard educational program. These small, student group activities fired university-level research, which has focused primarily on the issues of group leadership, impact of group membership on academic performance, and effect of group participation on success in later life (Strang, 1958).

Whether these group learning experiences take place in the public schools or in the college environment, the associated techniques can be used to support very different conceptions of knowledge. They can serve the traditional classroom, which focuses on the teacher as the source of knowledge and authority. They can also become an avenue for achieving learner empowerment and alter the fundamental role and function of the instructor (Bruffee, 1984). Thus, although there is nothing essentially revolutionary about the use of student group work in college classes, it is one way of achieving substantially radical ends. If we are fully to appreciate the potentially radical implications of such classroom practices for higher education, we must understand how conceptions of knowledge and authority inform the typical college classroom.

Knowledge and Authority in the Traditional Classroom

Once a class begins, the locus of knowledge and authority is usually quite apparent. As noted earlier, the instructor is the central character. What precedes the first day of class is perhaps less apparent. For example, the institutional policies, teacher training practices, criteria for class size, and assignment guidelines all combine to shape a course before it has begun. While it is clear that students are central to the process, if only in the sense that every class needs someone to be taught, their role is analogous to that of consumers in a market economy. Students select from, rather than design, the products that are offered. The usual college course exists in and is informed, shaped, and qualified by a social, political, and economic context that centers more on the institution and the instructor than on the student. The decisions made by the teacher are crucial in determining the ideas, skills, and information that are to be presented and the classroom atmosphere or climate in which this presentation is to take place.

While the system just described may seem antidemocratic, it is not necessarily bad. Institutional powers, privileged knowledge, and a controlled classroom atmosphere and climate can produce stimulating learning environments. "Students learn from the myriad of interpersonal stimulations and challenges that occur within the classroom . . . through the presentation of well-organized curricula, through the assistance of teachers who are knowledgeable about a subject, and by students carrying out learning routines that are at times repetitious and even boring. Moreover, learning can occur from a teacher's lecturing, from a structured library experience, through the use of a workbook, and from a student's reflections during solitude" (Schmuck and Schmuck, 1983, p. xvi).

Transferring Power to the Learner

We need to question the nature of learning that occurs in such solitary pursuits. Is the learning environment engendered by didactic practices optimal, or can it be improved by altering the structures of knowledge and authority that have served to define higher education in the United States? Many teachers have discovered that the very process of conceptualizing a course, designing a learning process, and enacting that design is itself an extremely powerful learning experience. As one teacher notes, "I realized that when I lectured I was the one who learned most. I was the one whose thinking skills were enhanced and whose creativity was stimulated. I played the active learner role; the student's role was passive" (Glassman, 1980, p. 31).

This statement suggests that having the active role in learning can have benefits for the learner that the passive acquisition of information lacks. Of course, there is ample evidence that people are more prone to learn subjects or questions that they have had an active role in framing (Freire, 1974). Active learning also implicates the learner's affective side. Although the acquisition of knowledge through cognitive processes is important, knowledge that remains merely cognitive may not make an individual able to function effectively. What is needed is a translation of knowledge so that it becomes genuinely significant in the experience of the learner. Active learning may provide a medium for such a translation. Active learning is epitomized by collaborative group work that replaces the "well-controlled" classroom with an active interpersonal environment (Schmuck and Schmuck, 1983, p. xv).

If intellectual conceptualization and classroom enactment based on it produce active and engaged learners, if the learning that results is more effective than the learning produced by the conventional didactic model, and if collaborative learning techniques foster this type of engaged, active learning, the question becomes, How can such learning environments be created and nurtured, and why are they not more common?

As noted earlier, the use of student groups in the teaching-learning enterprise is neither new nor necessarily radical. The work of Slavin (1983) in particular illustrates that cooperative student learning does not pose a substantial threat to standard classroom structures (see also Johnson and Johnson, 1987; Cohen, 1986). That is to say, the proponents of cooperative learning strategies design group methods largely to complement, not challenge, the traditional structures. Such group activities reinforce the standard concept of teacher authority and build on the principle that classroom knowledge is something that students are to acquire, not create.

One can in fact define *cooperative learning* (as opposed to collaborative learning) as the use of student learning groups to support an instructional system that maintains the traditional lines of classroom knowledge and authority. If cooperative learning techniques are conceptualized in this way, we see that they tend to help students learn discrete pieces of information that the instructor has already identified. As such, they are simply one more tool that can help the teacher to transmit curricular content to students.

A brief evaluation of some of the methods designed by Slavin (1983) will illustrate this point. The fact that the author just cited and others worked primarily with students at lower grade levels when developing their approaches to group learning processes does not necessarily limit the theoretical implications of their work. For example, Slavin (1983, p. 23) characterizes student team learning models as perhaps the "most extensively researched and widely used cooperative learning techniques" available.

One of these models, called Student Teams-Achievement Divisions (STAD), places students in small, heterogeneous groups representing a microcosm of the class. The teacher introduces the material by way of lecture or discussion. The teams study worksheets, work problems, quiz each other, or use some other means—whatever it takes to learn the concepts and master the material that has been assigned.

In STAD and the other strategies that Slavin (1983) describes, the teacher retains control over the information to be mastered and the atmosphere or climate of the classroom in which the mastery takes place.

Beyond Groups to Collaboration

In all the cooperative strategies just reviewed, students have the role of information receiver, not of knowledge creator. However, student group processes can be used to present a more basic challenge to the underlying precepts of the traditional college classroom. When used in such a context, student group activities become collaborative learning strategies. Under collaborative strategies, at least some aspects of classroom knowledge and authority can be developed or created both by students and teacher. The basic framework for the use of collaborative learning in college classes dates in the United Kingdom to the 1950s. In the United States, student learning groups did not begin to be used in college classrooms until the 1970s (Bruffee, 1984).

The American colleges that adopted these increasingly student-centered learning methods were driven more by pragmatism than by research results or an affinity for radical politics. The post–Vietnam era student body seemed to be substantially disengaged from the traditional forms of college-level classroom instruction. Student group learning methods were an experimental technique that seemed to engage students in the learning process by emphasizing its social context.

Like other sociopolitical institutions, the educational system is structured to resist revolutionary change: "The competitive nature of our colleges and universities, our system of evaluation, our past educational experiences, even our academic calendar (particularly the quarter system) all create obstacles to successful collaboration. The collaborative learning model, in fact, runs directly counter to our own professional training and reward system" (Ede, 1987, p. 8).

The use of collaborative learning techniques in the traditional college class-room could produce potentially radical change in two areas: the role of knowledge and the role of authority.

Knowledge: Who Decides

As noted earlier, the college instructor has historically exercised substantial control over the knowledge that is to be valued in his or her classroom. Each instructor decides what types of information, materials, ideas, and concepts are to be transmitted to students and how students' success in receiving them is to be evaluated. The instructor normally makes this decision in isolation—isolated from students if not also from disciplinary peers and institutional supervisors. The two types of knowledge that are most privileged in this context are disciplinary knowledge and pedagogical knowledge. I am emphatically not suggesting that there is an absolute or essential separation between what is taught in a course and how it is taught. Research shows that the methods we use to convey information teach as much as if not more than the information conveyed. I use these two concepts to identify focal points within largely overlapping systems so that we can concentrate on their individual effects and properties. By doing so, I do not mean to ignore their important interconnections.

Disciplinary knowledge is an understanding of the information, concepts, and so forth that are valued within the bounds of a traditional subject matter. From his or her position as scholar, the instructor is traditionally seen as being in the best position to know both of what this knowledge consists and which parts of it are appropriate for students to consume. Pedagogical knowledge is an awareness of the teaching techniques and strategies available to help students to acquire the appropriate disciplinary knowledge. Again, as the trained teaching professional, the instructor is traditionally seen as occupying the best position to make informed decisions about the appropriate instructional routes to follow. Collaborative learning can challenge both traditions.

As Thomas Kuhn (1970) observed of the sciences, the accepted epistemological structures—the foundations and organization of the received knowledge within a particular discipline—are not necessarily either the only or even the best way of conceptualizing the tremendous array of ideas, information, concepts, and "facts" that inform the discipline. At the same time, those structures are considered to be "standard" in large measure because the paradigms that support them are so widely accepted. A shift in the paradigm shifts the epistemological structure, and what was "accepted" disciplinary knowledge may suddenly not be accepted any longer. The reigning paradigm at any point in time is essentially the product of agreement among the most important participants in the enterprise—what Kenneth A. Bruffee (1986, p. 773) calls "communities of like-minded peers." Thus, disciplinary knowledge is the child of paradigmatic structures that at bottom are socially constructed.

Viewed in this way, the "privileged" knowledge of the instructor looks somewhat different. If knowledge is socially constructed, the important intersections of thought and action are not those that take place between an individual and, for example, a canonical text but rather those that occur among the members of a community of knowledgeable peers. From this perspective, knowledge and the authority that knowledge commands are generated and maintained (Bruffee, 1986) by the community. Collaborative learning, then, can be seen as the hand that fits ever so snugly into the glove of social constructivism. "Collaborative learning is related to social construction in that it assumes learning occurs among persons rather than between a person and things. Some teachers using collaborative learning who have adopted social constructionist assumptions have found that they understand better what they are trying to do and, understanding better, have a better chance of doing it well" (Bruffee, 1986, p. 787).

These notions of how knowledge is formed have the potential for altering classroom practice in radical ways. If a small group of students working together can act as a community of knowledgeable peers, then the group can construct knowledge. The teacher is no longer a repository of the "right" answers. Although the instructor may well know what answers a given discipline deems to be "acceptable," the students themselves can generate a repertoire of answers that the community represented by the classroom accepts. Using collaborative learning processes, they can rely on their own expertise, their own interactions, and their own prior understandings to create new knowledge.

Assuming that the collaborative project progresses to this point, other questions must be asked. For example, of what value or use is the knowledge generated by a class of "knowledgeable peers"? What is the relationship between the forms of disciplinary knowledge that the instructor possesses and the other types of created and experiential knowledge that students possess? How can the instructor and the members of the class outside a particular collaborative group access the knowledge that a group has generated? What prior knowledge does a group need in order to generate new knowledge? If the members of a group are not exposed to the "accepted" structures of disciplinary knowledge, can they even ask questions capable of generating new knowledge? These questions have yet to be answered.

But we are progressing too quickly. These questions presume that the collaborative learning process has worked. However, if anything is certain, it has to be that collaborative learning does not simply occur when an instructor places several students together and asks them to work together on an assignment. As with any other instructional method, it takes crafting. In fact, because collaborative learning runs counter to many of the traditional norms of college teaching, careful, self-conscious crafting may be absolutely necessary. As one observer has noted, "Probably the most important requirement [for effective small-group learning] is a supportive climate that reduces resistance to learning. The process of changing one's patterns of thought and behavior is difficult, and a climate that reduces individual defensiveness and anxiety about exposure is paramount in overcoming resistance to learning. The purpose is . . . to create a supportive atmosphere which will encourage [the student] to undertake the task of learning, to cope with anxieties and concerns, and to experiment with new ways of thinking and behaving. Development of a supportive atmosphere requires at least two essential conditions within the learning situation: First, threat must be minimized. The climate must be such that defensiveness is reduced. Second, emotional support must be provided while the learner is undergoing change in thinking and action" (Strang, 1958, p. 84).

Authority: Who Rules

This is true, or at least it sounds good, but is tension in the learning environment always something to be avoided? The teacher should be cognizant of the traditional mechanisms of control and authority present in the college classroom—mechanisms that favor individual over group effort, competition over cooperation, and teacher-directed over student-directed learning. The instructor must consciously construct an atmosphere that reverses or at least modifies the probable effects of these structures that can affect the collaborative process in negative ways. Simply ignoring these structures is not enough.

Students have succeeded in twelve years of prior schooling, so they do not come to the college classroom as educational neophytes. They have certain knowledge about the classroom, certain expectations about the use of power and authority in the classroom. But, as the earlier discussion of the institutional context in which the college classroom operates implied, aspects of the traditional authority structure cannot be avoided. The instructor cannot entirely reconstruct either the culture or the learning institution. At best, the instructor can take positive steps to redirect the traditional sources of authority. But clearly, regarding the authority structures that can be changed, the teacher must not only "free" his or her own mind but communicate that freedom to the students as well.

As Bosworth points out in Chapter Three of this volume, for collaborative learning to operate effectively, the proper conditions must be present. The instructor must use personal knowledge and authority to change the relatively contrived environment that is the college classroom into a learning environment. "For maximum change to occur, a group must possess . . . a learning culture. In permanently structured groups, these ingredients may already be present. However, in most instructional situations, where students usually meet for short periods spread over weeks or months, instructors must create and develop the requisite structure and processes of the group" (Olmstead, 1974, p. 92).

To maximize the possibility of success with collaborative processes, the instructor must understand the operational premises of these processes. These premises include an awareness that a group of reasonably capable adults can learn on its own if the instructor will let it, that it is not essential for an instructor to control every input into the discussion in order for the discussion to be an effective learning experience, and that maximum learning probably occurs when a group breaks its dependence on its instructor and assumes its own responsibility for learning (Olmstead, 1974).

The teacher cannot abdicate or completely abandon his or her authority, but there can be a conscious and, it is to be hoped, a skillful redeployment (Cohen, 1986). Some traditional forms of classroom control can reappear in other guises. While groups can operate to foster active learners, help to shift the responsibility for learning away from the instructor and toward the student, and perhaps even generate new knowledge, they can also create powerful pressures on their members that thwart these possibilities. Tyranny can prevail within a group just as it can under an instructor. The instructor must be vigilant to ensure that the leadership patterns within collaborative groups allow for the instructional goals that he or she has established to be realized.

Conclusion

Collaborative learning requires an authoritative instructional presence if it is to be successful. However, the role of the teacher in exercising such authority is substantially different from his or her role when using didactic teaching strategies. For collaborative learning, instructors must set up the process and facilitate its operation. In most cases, collaborative learning will not happen by itself. Instructors may need to draw on all their pedagogical knowledge and training to establish a collaborative classroom atmosphere. Once groups are operating, the instructor may also need to draw on his or her knowledge of the discipline to guide group inquiry. However, this knowledge needs to be used as a basis for posing investigatory or generative questions, not for supplying the "correct" answers to students' inquiries. One cannot simply throw students together with their peers with no guidance or preparation and expect a successful collaborative learning experience to result. In fact, to do this would most likely be to perpetuate, perhaps even aggravate, the prevailing negative effects of peer group influences: conformity, anti-intellectualism, intimidation, and a drop in quality. To counteract these possibilities requires the instructor to create and maintain a demanding academic environment, one that makes collaboration a genuine part of students' educational development (Bruffee, 1984).

References

Bruffee, K. A. "Collaborative Learning and the 'Conversation of Mankind.'" *College English,* 1984, *46,* 635–652.

Bruffee, K. A. "Social Construction, Language, and the Authority of Knowledge: A Bibliographical Essay." *College English,* 1986, *48* (8), 773–790.

Cohen, E. G. *Designing Groupwork: Strategies for the Heterogeneous Classroom.* New York: Teachers College Press, 1986.

Ede, L. "The Case for Collaboration." Paper presented at the College Composition and Communication Conference, Atlanta, 1987.

Freire, P. *Pedagogy of the Oppressed.* New York: Seabury Press, 1974.

Giroux, H. A., and Simon, R. I. "Popular Culture as Pedagogy of Pleasure and Meaning." In H. A. Giroux and R. I. Simon (eds.), *Popular Culture: Schooling and Everyday Life.* New York: Bergin and Garvey, 1989.

Glassman, E. "The Teacher as Leader." In K. E. Eble (ed.), *Improving Teaching Styles.* San Francisco: Jossey-Bass, 1980.

Johnson, D. W., and Johnson, R. *Learning Together and Alone.* Englewood Cliffs, N.J.: Prentice Hall, 1987.

Kuhn, T. S. *The Structure of Scientific Revolutions.* (2nd ed.) Chicago: University of Chicago Press, 1970.

Olmstead, J. A. *Small-Group Instruction: Theory and Practice.* Alexandria, Va.: Resources Research Organization, 1974.

Schmuck, R. A., and Schmuck, P. A. *Group Processes in the Classroom.* (4th ed.) Dubuque, Iowa: Brown, 1983.

Slavin, R.E. *Cooperative Learning.* New York: Longman, 1983.

Strang, R. *Group Work in Education.* New York: Harper, 1958.

JAMES L. FLANNERY *teaches social studies and tries to use collaborative learning methodologies at Blooming High School South.*

This chapter identifies the social skills needed for effective collaborative learning and describes strategies that can enhance students' collaborative skill.

Developing Collaborative Skills in College Students

Kris Bosworth

My freshman year in college, I roomed with a woman from another community. We both had done very well in high school, had made national honor society our junior year, and won small scholarships. We had succeeded at playing the competitive academic game for twelve years. We carried that competition into the college environment by becoming very competitive with each other. As freshmen, we took several of the same courses. The unspoken rule was to do better than the other on tests and on papers.

Our competitive training from high school did not allow us even to discuss the ideas and concepts we were learning in courses. We did not study together, quiz each other on concepts before a test, or practice speeches or presentations with each other. For us, feedback inherently meant criticism. Criticism was permitted only from faculty or upperclassmen—anyone whom we defined as being in a position to be "better" than we were.

—Pat, a senior at a small liberal arts college

College instructors face a dilemma when they use collaborative strategies in their classrooms. How can collaboration be successful if the students do not have the skills or in many cases even the desire to participate in collaborative activities?

In the traditional academic setting, where individuals compete for grades and academic standing, cooperation and collaboration are usually not rewarded. In such a setting, the instructor expert is seen as possessing superior knowledge and wisdom, and he or she sits in judgment on the ideas and abilities of the student novice. From the student's point of view, such a system is characterized by a narrow focus on one's own work, the sometimes destructive criticism of the work of others (after all, they are the competition), the sharing of ideas only with power figures, manipulation of the system to one's own benefit where possible, and a general lack of trust. In marked contrast, collaboration involves cooperation and compromise, flexibility in roles, trust and respect for others, questions as well as criticism, and group problem solving.

Most of the students who enter college are products of the competition model. Their high school experience has reinforced their naturally competitive instincts. In fact, the students whom we are most likely to find in a college classroom are the ones who have been most successful at competitive academics. Their urge to compete and their success at it have led them to campus. Through high school, there has been little room for or experience with collaboration. Like any other skill that has not been practiced, their cooperative skills have become rusty.

Consequently, when these students find themselves in a college-level collaborative learning environment, they often resist the collaborative process or engage in it only minimally. When college instructors, who are not always familiar with collaborative learning processes, encounter such a response, they often attribute it either to the presumed inadequacies of collaborative learning itself or to their own inadequacy in its methods. However, resistance to collaboration can often be attributed to one or the other of two factors: students' use of inappropriate skills or students' lack of appropriate skills (Schultz, 1990). For example, a group may get off to a slow start if everyone is competing with each other, jockeying for leadership positions, or unwilling to listen to each other or to share ideas. These competitive activities increase the time that it takes for the group to begin to work together productively, and it can jeopardize the quality of the end product. Perhaps a more common result of inadequate collaborative skills is that work among members of the work group is unbalanced. In an unbalanced group, the distribution of work is unequal, and some members feel that they are doing more than their share. While an emphasis on individual accountability can remedy the imbalance structurally, inadequate interpersonal skills may prevent the group from identifying the cause of the problem. For example, a group member may not be assertive enough to identify overwork, or group members may not be good at communicating what each task involves. No matter what the reason or the precise nature of the breakdown in the collaborative process, the result is the same: Student learning is impeded.

This chapter describes the role of collaborative interpersonal and social skills in the facilitation of successful collaborative processes in the college classroom. A taxonomy of collaborative skills is identified, and a process for teaching these skills explicitly is outlined.

Taxonomy of Collaborative Skills

Collaborative skills form the framework in which collaborative learning can take place. Table 3.1 is a taxonomy of skills that facilitate collaboration in college classrooms. As Table 3.1 shows, some skills are prerequisites for good collaborative work, while others grow and are nurtured through practice in a collaborative environment.

Interpersonal Skills. Interpersonal skills are the basic social skills that most college students learn through interaction with friends and family and in social situations. They include being interested in getting to know someone's name, being able to listen to another person, giving constructive rather than destructive feedback, responding to another person's idea and not just the person, and abstaining from put-downs and derogatory comments. In the collaborative process, these skills must be present if rapport is to be established among group members. They are essential throughout the process if group interaction is to remain smooth.

Group Management Skills. In the traditional classroom, several activities occur. The instructor assumes the bulk of the responsibility for managing

Table 3.1. Taxonomy of Collaborative Skills

Skills Category	Collaborative Skills
Interpersonal skills	Congenial, friendly Make clear statements Listening skills Positive communication (no name calling, put-downs) Eye contact
Group building/management	Organize work Keep group on task Run a meeting Participate in group self-analysis Show empathy
Inquiry skills	Clarification Critique Probe assumptions and evidence Probe implication & consequences Elicit viewpoints & perspectives
Conflict	Prevention Resolution Mediation
Presentation	Summarize, synthesize Speaking in front of a group Creating presentation materials Report writing

the pace of the learning process. Individual students have to manage their own time on specific tasks, such as writing research papers. In the collaborative process, students take a substantial amount of control over the process by which they learn. Groups of students have to manage a variety of learning tasks, such as negotiating differences of perspective and arriving at consensus. Yet, before success can be achieved in these complex learning processes, students must know how to succeed collaboratively at the pragmatic level of group management. Essential group management skills include making and following an agenda, keeping on task, completing tasks on a deadline, showing empathy with the needs and problems of fellow group members, and discussing feelings about the group and the process.

Inquiry Skills. Students need inquiry skills in order to probe for additional information; analyze, synthesize, and evaluate information and findings; and draw conclusions. As such, these skills are essential if students are to seek information from a variety of sources and to evaluate the information and the sources. Use of these skills is not unique to collaborative classrooms, but it is critical to the success of collaborative activities.

Conflict Resolution Skills. Conflict is struggle resulting from incompatible or opposing needs, drives, wishes, or external or internal demands. Conflicts can arise in groups over such interpersonal issues as a member's not having his or her work done for a group meeting, or they can be intellectual because group members cannot agree on an interpretation or a mode of presentation. Although thoughtful attention to structure and organization can prevent some common conflicts, any serious collaboration is certain to engender a certain amount of conflict. Group members must have the skills needed to resolve such conflicts productively.

Synthesis and Presentation Skills. The ability to synthesize information is crucial to the effective presentation of ideas. Once a group has gathered information, group members need to decide how best to organize, synthesize, and present it so that others can understand and appreciate their findings. An effective presentation requires group members to agree on an appropriate approach, carry through on it, and bring it to closure. Essential to developing the group's approach are the skills of synthesizing and evaluating information and identifying evidence that supports or refutes claims. Basic writing and speaking skills become important at this stage, but skills in drama, videography, and art can transform an acceptable presentation into an exceptional one.

Teaching Collaborative Skills

The taxonomy of collaborative skills presented in Table 3.1 includes guidelines for instructors who design lessons, syllabi, and curricula for collaborative learning environments. Clearly, such skills as active listening and speaking permeate all the categories. Students coming from a traditionally competitive academic background bring varied skill levels to their college classroom. In many cases, they may understand little of these five different skill types that they might be utilizing in academic settings. However, our college-level students bring with them experience in a wide range of nonacademic social relationships that draw on and develop these social skills and that thereby create a reservoir of tacit knowledge that instructors can tap.

Hence, the skills that students need for successful collaborative learning are already implicit in their past social experiences, and they need primarily to be made explicit. The process of making these collaborative skills explicit can be compared to construction scaffolding. In the initial stages of a project, builders set up a temporary structure to support their activity. Without such a structure, they can only build so high, and the risk of falls and other injuries is increased. However, by its very nature and purpose, scaffolding is only temporary. As the building takes shape and the inner and outer walls are put into place, the need for the scaffolding diminishes. When the structure is able to stand independently, the scaffolding is removed.

For some students, it may be enough simply to identify the collaborative social skills necessary for successful collaboration; these students need to be encouraged only to practice these skills in the classroom. For other students, different approaches might be warranted. Helping students to learn collaborative skills is similar to teaching other, more familiar skills, such as driving a car. Few of us would give the keys to our car to an individual who has taken one driving lesson and ask him or her to drive to Chicago. Such a trip involves a complex set of skills. Yet these skills can be taught through modeling and learned through practice. Instructors may need to model strategies for the class or ask individual groups to model particular strategies. The showing of videos about students engaged in collaborative learning processes can provide both motivation and examples (Hamilton, 1990; Bosworth and Welsh, 1993).

Cognitive psychologists have demonstrated the differences between the thinking processes of experts and the thinking processes of novices accomplishing the same task, such as playing chess or driving a car (Dreyfus and Dreyfus, 1986; Anderson, 1985). Chapter 9 of this sourcebook describes an expansion of the model presented by Dreyfus and Dreyfus (1986).

Fits and Posner (1967) identified three levels of skill acquisition that can help us to understand students' development as collaborative learners.

In the first stage, novices perform the task by rigidly following specific rules and then modify the rules as they become accustomed to working collaboratively. The scaffolding is firmly in place.

In the second stage, misunderstandings of the rules are identified and eliminated, relationships between various rules and situations become clear, and students learn how to plan actions, anticipate problems that can arise, and take preventive measures.

In the third stage, spontaneity increases, and students become able to respond automatically to a variety of collaborative learning conditions. The scaffolding has been removed.

Thus, once students know the rules or procedures for a particular skill, they can, with practice and feedback, develop competence and confidence in their ability to work collaboratively.

Study of the literature in cognitive psychology on novices and experts helps to clarify how instructors can enable students to gain the social skills necessary for successful learning through collaboration. Helping students to develop collaborative skills involves, first, understanding that each student comes into the classroom at a different skill level.

Strategies for Teaching Collaborative Skills

The strategies that we use to teach the skills necessary for collaborative learning are not unlike the skills that we use to teach other skills. Teaching collaborative skills needs to be planned with the same care as teaching any other content.

Identification of Skills. The first step is for the instructor to become familiar with the collaborative skills that will be needed for a particular activity to be successful in his or her classroom. Experience with preceding classes may indicate the specific skills that need to be sharpened for success in any particular course. By observing students during the first week of class, instructors can also identify the areas of weakness and strength for individuals.

Suggestion. Videotaping five to ten minutes of a group working together on a focused problem or task and having the group then review the tape can help its members to identify the essential skills.

Demonstration of Skill. Once the skills have been identified and the order in which they are to be introduced has been determined, the instructor exposes the class to examples of the skill as it is to be used in the classroom. The identified skill needs to be clarified with the learner. The learner needs to understand what that skill is, why it is important, and what a person who is making use of it looks or sounds like.

Suggestion. The instructor can pull examples from work that students already have done. Or the instructor can give a series of examples of what students or student work looks or sounds like. For relatively complex skills, such as conflict resolution, the instructor can set up a role play in which students demonstrate the use of the skill.

Modeling. Throughout classroom interactions with students, the teacher models skills for them. Often, it can be helpful for the instructor to talk his or her way through the use of a skill that he or she is modeling. This reflection helps students to understand the kinds of mental decisions that the individual makes when practicing the skill.

Suggestion. If students are at the first stage of rule learning, the instructor can break individual skills down into behavioral steps. For example, the steps in keeping a group on task can include defining the task clearly, setting an agenda, agreeing to complete the agenda, setting a time frame, monitoring time and progress on agenda, and reminding group members of time and agenda.

Performance Feedback. Students need opportunities to practice skills in the classroom and receive feedback from their peers and the instructor. Because students may not be familiar with some skills or because these skills may differ significantly from what students are accustomed to in a more competitive environment, instructors need to coach students by rewarding positive behavior and correcting unskillful behavior. Classmates can also give feedback. Feedback serves to reinforce practice of these skills in the collaborative process.

Suggestion. At the end of a group session, each group can evaluate the effectiveness and utility of a particular skill to achieve their collaborative task. If more than one skill is being practiced, a checklist supplied by the instructor might be a useful format.

Reflection. A critical component in the learning process is time to process and reflect on one's experiences. Instructors need to give students an opportunity to talk about their experiences and discuss how they can improve their effectiveness. Students can share examples of various skills and discuss the dilemmas that they faced when they tried to apply these skills in a collaborative learning environment. As in other steps, instructor modeling is an important part of the process.

Suggestion. Some instructors have used a self-evaluation questionnaire at the end of each class. The questionnaire asks students to reflect on their progress in adopting the collaborative skill or skills of focus. This feedback can help the instructor to determine how fast the class is moving and identify questions or dilemmas arising from practice of the new skills.

Summary

Although one benefit of collaborative learning is improved social and collaborative skills, instructors cannot assume that the students coming into college classrooms have the skills that they need to begin a collaborative process. This chapter has identified the kinds of collaborative skills that students need and described some strategies that instructors can use to teach these skills explicitly.

References

Anderson, J. R. *Cognitive Psychology and Its Implications.* New York: W. H. Freeman, 1985.

Bosworth, K., and Welsh, T. "Design and Evaluation of an Interactive Multimedia Program for Teacher Education." *Journal of Technology and Teacher Education,* 1993, *1* (1), 15–23.

Dreyfus, H. C., and Dreyfus, S. E. *Mind over Machine: The Power of Human Intuition and Expertise in the Era of the Computer.* New York: Free Press, 1986.

Fits, P. M., and Posner, M. I. *Human Performance.* Belmont, Calif.: Brooks/Cole, 1967.

Hamilton, S. "Collaborative Learning: Workshop" (videotape). Urbana, Ill.: NCTE, 1990.

Schultz, J. L. "Cooperative Learning: Refining the Process." *Educational Leadership,* 1990, *47,* 43–45.

KRIS BOSWORTH is assistant professor in curriculum and instruction and director of the Center for Adolescent Studies at Indiana University.

This chapter describes an experimental course in introductory biology and its relation to individual learning styles and raises issues of group dynamics in collaborative learning.

Group Dynamics: Understanding Group Success and Failure in Collaborative Learning

Judith E. Miller, John Trimbur, John M. Wilkes

Group work invariably produces tensions that are normally absent, unnoticed, or suppressed in traditional classes. Students bring with them a variety of personality types, cognitive styles, and expectations about their own role in the classroom and their relationship with the teacher, peers, and the subject matter of the course. As a result, students may well experience confusion and even anxiety about the work in a collaborative classroom and about how they will be evaluated. This chapter suggests some conceptual tools that teachers will find useful in thinking about the processes of collaboration in their own classrooms.

In this chapter, we describe an experimental biology course in order to raise issues of group dynamics in collaborative learning. The course is an introductory class for biology majors that largely replaces traditional lectures and tests with small-group problem-solving activities. Results from the past four years of experience suggest that we are succeeding in encouraging students to view science as the application of a body of knowledge to a collaborative process of organized investigation, not just a mass of facts to be memorized. At the same time, curricular reform of the type described here puts new pressure on students to work together effectively in small groups and to master unfamiliar types of learning tasks.

Course Background

Since spring 1989, Miller and her colleague Ronald Cheetham have offered Biology I and II in an active learning format at Worcester Polytechnic Institute

NEW DIRECTIONS FOR TEACHING AND LEARNING, no. 59, Fall 1994   © Jossey-Bass Publishers

(WPI). Each course spans seven weeks. Each week, there are two "lectures" accommodating the entire course enrollment, which runs from forty to seventy students, and two conference meetings for sixteen to eighteen students. Each problem spans about six class meetings (one and a half weeks). All meetings are devoted to problem-related activities. The course faculty write the problem statements, sometimes with reference to a unifying theme for the term (for example, design of a closed life-support system for long-term space flight; the question of whether Vietnam veterans should be compensated for exposure to Agent Orange), sometimes with reference to questions and topic areas generated by students that have been funneled through a student curriculum committee. Typical classroom activities include two overview lectures of no more than thirty minutes each; small-group discussion of sections of the problem; structured collaborative learning activities; informal oral progress reports; quizzes; and formal student oral reports. Students, in groups of four or five members each, are expected to do the bulk of their research, meeting, and writing outside class. Written and oral problem reports, both of which are group products, account for more than half of the course grade. The grades that students receive for their individual written reports depend heavily on evaluations by their fellow group members, so group dynamics issues are prominent. Miller and Cheetham (1990) and Goodwin, Miller, and Cheetham (1991) describe course design, operation, and initial student response.

The Impact of Group Dynamics. Initially, course instructors were surprised to find that the process-related issue of group dynamics consumed as much or more faculty effort than issues related to content. The personal and working relationships within the small groups can either make or break the course experience for many students. Some groups literally crackle with excitement and creativity. All members seem to live, breathe, eat, and sleep the current project and are ecstatic with their working arrangements ("I love my group!"). Members of these groups can develop close friendships that last for their entire undergraduate careers and vocally resist being broken up as groups are rearranged. At the opposite end of the spectrum, there are groups in which one or more members cannot be reached by telephone, do not show up for meetings, break commitments to their group, and in the worst case disappear for several weeks with the entire group's work in their possession. In this course, there have been groups in which one or two people have carried the whole group, groups that ejected individual members, groups in which there was continual conflict for seven weeks, groups in which harmonious mediocrity prevailed, and groups in which everyone seemed satisfied with an uneven division of labor. Some groups degenerate after a strong start. Others resolve their initial conflicts and work well from then on.

The group scenarios just sketched can have a tremendous impact on the success or failure of the learning environment. The differences among them are therefore of interest to teachers for their impact on three criteria: performance, harmony, and satisfaction.

Performance. Individual learning is one of the most important criteria for gauging the success of a collaborative learning format. Group grades on the written and oral reports are measures of both collaborative work skills and of individual performance. Hence we have added other measures, such as quiz grades and grades in subsequent biology courses, to get at individual learning. To identify individual contributions to the group products, students grade (in privacy) the contribution of group members to each project at its end.

Harmony. We want the students to learn to appreciate diversity, and indeed that is one documented benefit of collaborative learning tasks (Slavin, 1980; Sharan, 1984). Although harmony and performance are not synonymous, excessive conflict can certainly interfere with performance. Paradoxically, excessive harmony can do the same, because the members of the best groups tend to be critical of one another's work or at least to tolerate an in-house critic; they tend also to impose high standards on themselves. The main measures of group harmony are derived from questionnaires that individual students fill out at the end of each problem. These questionnaires yield patterns of relationship assessments within individual groups. There is also one direct item about group harmony.

Satisfaction. Since one of our major objectives in organizing the course in the way described here is to generate excitement about the study of biology, we are interested in student satisfaction, especially as it affects retention in the major. We derive measures of overall learning satisfaction from questionnaires administered before and after each course (Goodwin, Miller, and Cheetham, 1991) and from students' responses on WPI's standard course evaluation form. We have measured group satisfaction—more precisely, perceived group effectiveness—from responses to a series of items on questionnaires administered at the end of each problem.

Approaches to Thinking About Group Dynamics

The performance, harmony, and satisfaction that collaborative learning seeks to foster are, of course, rarely achieved through a smooth and unimpeded process. Group work can be a messy and uneven business, and teachers need to distinguish between student responses to collaborative learning that are signs of growth and responses that signal barriers to development. To that end, this section reviews three models that we have found useful in thinking about group success and failure. Each model brings certain aspects of collaborative learning into view.

Personality and Learning Style. As an approach to characterizing personality in ways that illuminate both group dynamics and learning styles, the most mature body of thought centers on the Jungian theory of personality operationalized by the Myers-Briggs Type Inventory (MBTI). This is a standard measure, available from Consulting Psychologists Press (Myers, 1991), which takes about twenty minutes to administer. In the context of learning styles,

McCormick (1992) has provided a useful breakdown. Figure 4.1 shows the learning style implications of the four dimensions of the MBTI.

Each person is scored on all four dimensions of the MBTI. Binary scoring on each of the four dimensions produces sixteen possible personality types. Although we have found it difficult to analyze MBTI data for so many individual types from a single class rigorously, we can characterize the flavor of an entire class. Our general biology students are predominantly introverts (59 percent), intuitives (66 percent), and thinkers (64 percent). Interestingly, this configuration resembles that of the scientific community at large, which tends to be disproportionately introverted, intuitive, and thinking, and contrasts with that of the general population, which tends to be extroverted, sensing, and feeling. The fourth dimension, Judging-Perceiving, is about evenly distributed in the general population and in our class (55 percent Perceiving).

The classic introverted intuitive thinking and perceiving individual is described as "rational, curious, theoretical, abstract," and one who prefers to "organize ideas rather than situations or people" (Hirsh and Kummerov, 1990, p. 29). Preferred work environments are described as "independent," "private," "flexible," "quiet," and "unstructured" (Hirsh and Kummerov, 1990, p. 29). This class distribution suggests that group-centered active learning could be a hard sell in that it conflicts with the inclination and self-image of a significant number of students.

MBTI theory stresses the need for balance in all groups, no matter what the task. However, such is hard to come by in a class so heavily skewed from the start. Since most learning style theory emphasizes the central functions of Thinking-Feeling and Intuition–Sensing at the expense of the other dimensions, it is worth looking at the inclination of a heavily intuitive thinking class organized into task groups.

Figure 4.1. Learning Style Implications of the MBTI Dimensions

MBTI TYPES

	INTROVERSION (I) reflection, careful, work alone ↔	EXTROVERSION (E) discussion, trial and error, groups
MBTI DIMENSIONS	INTUITION (N) hunches, concepts, imagination ↔	SENSING (S) facts, applications, hands-on
	THINKING (T) logical, objective, cause and effect ↔	FEELING (F) relationships, values, process
	JUDGING (J) ordered, closure, formal ↔	PERCEIVING (P) discussion, flexible, informal

The intuitives prefer dealing with global issues first and to proceed in roundabout discussions that use the agenda simply as a starting point. Novel suggestions and imaginative solutions excite them. Thinkers like concise presentations, want to weigh the pros and cons of each alternative, and are best convinced by cool rational arguments referring to goals and objectives. These qualities in combination have the interesting effect of producing people who focus on the possibilities rather than the facts at hand but also cut directly to the core issues, for good or ill. They seek to explain things in terms of models and theory at an abstract level.

A good case can be made that diversity on the two central dimensions (Intuition-Sensing and Thinking-Feeling) benefits most groups. Groups weighted toward intuitive thinking are likely to lapse in the areas of detail work (that is, double-checking and step-by-step follow-through) and sensitivity to the feelings of group members.

Despite the emphasis on Intuition and Thinking in learning style theory, they are the Judging-Perceiving and, to a lesser extent, the Introversion-Extroversion dimensions that most affect group harmony and provoke the kind of fundamental conflict that can disable a group before it even gets down to task. Moreover, similarities in these areas make for group harmony that influences student satisfaction with the course, although it may not show up in performance differentials.

Basically, the judgers work best in a structured and orderly environment and seek early closure on the plan of action. The perceivers like to defer decision in order to gather as much information as possible and preserve flexibility as long as possible. The Extroversion-Introversion dimension is significant, because the introverts are slower to speak; that is, they are ready to share only what is well thought out and only what they are committed to and prepared to defend. The extroverts literally think out loud and are less likely to be committed to their ideas. An introverted judger can think that the group has a consensus plan and start to implement it only to find that the extroverted perceiver comes into the next meeting with a whole new plan based on all the things that surfaced at the last meeting.

It is easy for people who play by the same rules to work harmoniously with each other. At the same time, however, conflicts born from diversity can promote intellectual negotiation and innovation and thereby enhance performance, although not necessarily satisfaction.

Cognitive Styles Model. The cognitive style typology (Gordon and Morse, 1969) that we adopted for this study derives from the literatures on organizational behavior and creativity. This approach has been applied usefully to the study of research styles in the past, but it has only recently been applied to the problem of learning styles. Gordon's cognitive typology (Gordon and Morse, 1969) is based on two dimensions: remote association and differentiation. The two are measured separately and are not highly correlated with one another.

Remote association (RA) is a gift for rapid, nonlogical, and intuitive recombination of given elements that accelerates the process of problem solving when the problem is known and the elements are known or accessible (Mednick, 1963). The elements do not have to be juxtaposed for high remote associators to be able to make the connection. However, these ingenious types often cannot logically derive or reconstruct the path by which they came to their conclusion. Often, it is others who prove that they have settled on the right or the best solution.

Differentiation (Diff) helps to identify people with the discriminating eye who pick up and often fixate on discrepancies in theory or empirical evidence and identify the fruitful question. People who score high on this quality display a capacity to work with messy subjective criteria. They are the masters of the ill-structured task environment.

The question remains, Can these typologies tell us anything interesting about student performance or satisfaction either as individuals or in groups? We have investigated the effects of cognitive style on group interaction in the context of the relationships among five variables: cognitive style mix, group harmony, group satisfaction, group performance, and task type.

We have found that the degree of structure in a curriculum causes it to appeal differently to the two cognitively opposite types: problem finders (high Diff, low RAT) and problem solvers (low Diff, high RAT). The problem finders prefer unstructured tasks and thematic integration of course topics, while the problem solvers favor a structured task environment. A third type, the implementer (low Diff, low RAT), also prefers relatively structured tasks, but this shows up at the level of his or her performance, not in the attraction that the course exerts. Surprisingly, there is almost no correlation (.06) between individual satisfaction with learning and individual performance as measured by grades.

Satisfaction with the group is highly dependent on group harmony. Nevertheless, group satisfaction does not improve with experience, that is, on sequential group tasks. Group harmony depends on cognitive style mix. Groups in which members are all integrators (high Diff, high RAT) or all implementors are the most harmonious (100 percent and 83 percent, respectively). Groups of all problem finders or all problem solvers are the least harmonious (50 percent). Groups that mix diverse types fall in the middle (71 percent).

Group performance is highly dependent on cognitive style mix, with type-diverse groups outperforming type-alike groups by a considerable margin overall. Our few groups consisting entirely of problem solvers performed very poorly. Groups consisting only of implementors performed far better on more structured than on less structured tasks. There is no correlation between group performance and group conflict or between group performance and group satisfaction.

To summarize, teachers are faced with a difficult trade-off when they form groups: Cognitive diversity increases group conflict and thus decreases satisfaction, but it also improves performance.

Group Life Model. Developed by social work professionals to conceptualize the working dynamics of mutual aid groups in settlement houses, homeless shelters, youth centers, family therapy, and so on, the group life model attempts to distill predictable stages of group development. Translated from social work into education, the group life model considers the classroom as a social structure that elaborates a set of roles by which responsibilities are allocated, decisions are reached, and relationships and communication patterns are established within a network of people.

In a seminal article on group life, Bennis and Shepard (1956) present a developmental model to explain how maturing groups move through two main phases, from dependence to interdependence, by resolving first their relationship to the group leader (or teacher) and second the relationships among their members. In the first phase, when the group is preoccupied with the leader's authority, members typically encounter three subphases: an initial stage of dependence in which group members, as a result of their past experience in groups and orientations toward authority, identify with or withdraw from the leader and the group; an intermediate stage of counterdependence characterized by disenchantment with the leader in which dependents continue to seek the leader's approval and counterdependents rebel against the leader; and a final stage of negotiation in which independents step forward to redefine the leader's role and the group begins to develop its own internal authority system. Negotiating the problem of how to deal with the leader's authority clears the way for members of the group to negotiate issues of intimacy and establish effective working relationships and communication.

The concern with intimacy constitutes the second main phase in the model proposed by Bennis and Shepard (1956), the phase of interdependence. Like the first stage, the second stage has three subphases that groups typically negotiate: an initial stage of enchantment in which the independence attained by rebelling against the leader promotes group harmony but also creates pressures for group conformity; an intermediate stage of disenchantment in which new ambivalence concerning the degree of intimacy required by the group emerges and scapegoating and struggles for leadership are typical; and a final stage of consensual validation in which the group clarifies interpersonal issues that were obstacles to group work and develops a group culture that tolerates alignment in subgroups, a stable status hierarchy, and leadership roles. At this point, members typically view the group as enabling their own purposes and fulfilling their needs.

There is a growing sense that, once project groups have been established in a class, they should not be shuffled or adjusted, as the growing-together process takes time. In the early stages, a group is no stronger than its strongest member (Michaelson, 1992). By the end, the group should be able to exceed the best effort of its strongest member. Thus, to shuffle is to prevent groups from maturing and to keep them dependent on the teacher. Certainly, the groups in our biology course resisted reshuffling, except for the groups that had expelled a member.

Practical Suggestions

Our intention in this section is to give teachers a beginning repertoire of practical suggestions that they can use to prevent and manage problems with group dynamics and that can help them to develop the fortitude needed to avoid feeling guilty about the variables that are not under their control. Each of the three approaches described in the preceding section—personality type, cognitive style, and the group life model—suggests strategies that teachers can use to try to optimize or at least balance performance, harmony, and satisfaction. Some of the variables that we discuss in this section do not lend themselves to analysis by the models that we have presented. Thus, the collection of strategies that follows is rather eclectic.

Variables That Teachers Have Little Power to Affect. It may be small comfort to teachers to know that many of the variables that influence group dynamics are beyond a teacher's control. The early phases of group development are especially susceptible to influence by situational or institutional constraints, such as class scheduling, the social calendar (for example, fraternity and sorority activities, homecoming weekend), the grading system, the physical space available in the classroom, and the movability of furniture. Advance attention to some of these variables can minimize their impact, but it will probably not bypass any of the difficult early stages of group development. In addition, students' motivation levels vary as a result of whether the course is required or elective and whether they are majoring in the discipline. We have found that the nonmajors in our biology course for majors are more likely than the majors to resent the intellectual and social effort involved in collaborative learning and to be the focus of group dynamics problems.

Moreover, groups do not immediately improve with experience on the second task. Many deteriorate, and teachers must have faith that in time they will pull out of their tailspin. Intervening immediately to shuffle the groups can set them back, lose hard-won experience, and force them to start all over again.

Students bring with them a set of attitudes toward group work, teachers' roles, the competing claims of cooperation and competition, and intellectual work that are far more influential in their educational experience than a few hours a week in class. Although we might hope that our course can change the course of a student's intellectual future, the effects are manifest only months or years later on the rare occasions when it does. So being patient with ourselves is a corollary of being patient with group process and of giving groups the time and opportunity needed to recoup.

Teachers need to understand the limits of their ability to make groups work together successfully. Teachers can organize students into groups, assign tasks, and offer direction along the way. But the students themselves must connect to form an effective working group. Overall, teachers need to accept that many variables are beyond their control and that no group work experience will ever be perfect. An awareness of these variables can enable teachers to dissect problems as they arise; to identify, without guilt, components of the problems around which a solution must be worked; and to help the students diagnose the nature of their problem and the larger significance of their experience.

Variables That Teachers Can Address in Course Design. The second category of variables, those that teachers can address during the process of designing the course, includes students' prior intellectual and academic background, their personality types and cognitive styles, and their orientation toward group life. Teachers cannot, of course, predict the exact configuration of these variables among the members of a particular class. (In fact, we have found that the dominant cognitive type in our biology course is a moving target from year to year.) What teachers can do is to learn how the design and sequencing of tasks over a term can accommodate the range of students' intellectual abilities and academic backgrounds, personality types and cognitive styles, and orientation toward authority and intimacy. We have often made the mistake of devising open-ended assignments (for example, the task of designing a closed life-support system for long-term space flight mentioned earlier) that students were not able to define as a specific problem or feel confident about developing solutions and of using these assignments on a class that needed structure, especially at the outset. Nevertheless, we have had success in developing assignments from articles in the popular press about current scientific dilemmas or advances. Relevance was then automatically established, and since pragmatic application is an important part of the local student culture, the result was broad engagement with the course exercises.

Although teachers cannot influence personality type, cognitive style, or past experience in groups, knowledge of these variables can help them to design an array of tasks that enables every student to be in his or her element at least some of the time. Thus, it is important to create situations in which every student can on occasion shine, so that all students remain engaged, not just the students whose cognitive style matches the teacher's. It is important to create opportunities enabling every student to earn the respect of the members of his or her group. It is also important to create situations in which every student can be stretched, at least some of the time. One form of stretching is learning collaborative work skills. Another is the challenge of intellectual tasks that are not the student's forte. We have found that three strategies are useful in designing assignments that mix tasks so as to fulfill these objectives.

The first is to write assignments with multiple parts. Each part consists of a different type of task, for example, framing, conceptualization, analysis, synthesis, logical extension. Students will naturally divide up the questions to maximize their own comfort levels. Teachers might consider formalizing task assignments within groups so that tasks of a given type, such as analysis, rotate among group members from one assignment to another.

The second is to give students choices between tasks: Answer question 1 or question 2; evaluate the experiment of author X, or devise an experiment of your own. This strategy lets students deal from their strengths, at least at the outset, when confidence building requires an early success.

The third is to vary task type during the course, starting with less complex and more structured material and moving toward more complex and less structured material. This strategy helps the students who favor a more structured task environment to become accustomed to collaborative work and settle in with their group before they are faced with a task that is difficult for them.

Variables That Teachers Can Manipulate as the Course Progresses. There is more opportunity for intervention and negotiation among the variables that teachers can manipulate. Teachers can intervene when group dynamics falter, and they can call attention to their own role in the classroom and how it differs from traditional classroom teaching in order to help students redefine their relationship to the teacher's authority. The syllabus itself can be renegotiated as determined by the students' progress and interests. Teachers can raise metacognitive issues by asking students not only what but how they are learning and how the style of learning in a collaborative classroom differs from that in traditional classrooms.

Teachers can control the composition of working groups. We have used a variety of techniques to assign students to groups: (somewhat) random selection; compatibility of schedules for out-of-class meeting times as determined by a one-page questionnaire completed on the first day of class; and cognitive style, either to maximize or minimize the cognitive diversity within a group. We have never allowed students to choose their own groups, because we wish to create heterogeneous groups so as to foster the tolerance of diversity, especially with respect to science background and English proficiency. However, we have allowed students to express confidentially their preferences about those with whom they would particularly like and not like to work, and we honor those preferences (especially the negative ones) to the degree possible. We have kept groups together both for three and a half weeks (half the term) and for seven (the full term—our current preference).

Although most teachers are understandably reluctant to spend valuable class time discussing group process, we suggest that the student disengagement that results from major problems in group dynamics makes the investment of one class period in group work skills well worthwhile. We should teach the skills that we are grading. Thus, such a session should include a briefing on the necessity for and logistics of good communication and organization and give participants an opportunity to discuss the various kinds of talents and individual differences or preferences that different people bring to tasks. You could give students practice in these skills with a participatory exercise requiring them to work in small groups to solve a simple puzzle and then to reflect on and discuss the group process. Role plays of group meetings, with class discussion of successful aspects and areas for improvement, are another possibility.

We strongly recommend keeping groups together even when they have problems, because it is in this situation that students can develop their skills in negotiating differences. A teacher can help by encouraging and helping students to work things out among themselves. It never ceases to amaze us that, in 99 percent of the cases in which a student complains to us about a group dynamics problem, he or she has not seriously discussed the issue with the other members of the group. Our usual response is to coach the student on productive strategies for confrontation, such as I-messages (Gordon, 1975); to encourage the student to initiate the discussion; and to let us know how it goes. If that approach fails (which rarely happens), we offer to mediate a group meeting focused on the problem. Only as a last resort do we break up a group to resolve a group dynamics problem, and we have done it only once in five years.

At WPI, we are currently experimenting with the use of undergraduate peer learning assistants (PLAs) to work one on one with student groups. Early indications are that the PLAs have been extremely effective in helping students to improve both group process and group dynamics.

Conclusion

When we teach in the lecture mode, we make the questionable assumption that students are satisfied in direct proportion to their learning. Collaborative learning requires students to participate actively and perform cognitive and social tasks that are new and often difficult. It is not surprising that students do not always greet this experience with unalloyed enthusiasm: Remember that they are the masters of the traditional system and that we are changing the rules on them. The harder the task looks at the outset, the greater may be their discomfort, but the task has to look hard if it is to be a worthy challenge. The trade-off extends to group dynamics: Group harmony often correlates inversely with group performance but directly with satisfaction. Teachers face a tough choice about course objectives: What combination of performance, harmony, and satisfaction do we wish to optimize? Teachers who must make this decision cannot help but be influenced by the faculty reward system, which does not always encourage experimentation.

Teachers sometimes become discouraged when collaborative learning does not work smoothly. As we mentioned at the outset of this chapter, teachers sometimes blame themselves for problems that in fact are beyond their control. At other times, teachers blame students for not having the maturity and responsibility needed to carry out collaborative learning effectively. In such instances, teachers would do well to reflect that students probably do not have much direct prior experience to draw on and that they will not know spontaneously how to apply group experience from family or sports to the challenge of collaborative work in the classroom. We urge teachers, including ourselves, not to be discouraged by failures but instead to analyze why groups succeed and fail and to let the participants grow through their experience. Teachers need to be lenient in terms of processing time but not of standards or expectations.

Teachers can influence only some of the variables that affect group success and group failure, but an awareness of all the variables will enable them to increase their influence over the whole educational environment. Conflict in groups is inevitable, and it should be viewed as giving students a valuable opportunity to learn group work skills and appreciate both the value and the problems of diversity. The difficulties of collaborative learning are real. Nonetheless, one of its most important benefits is that it integrates social and intellectual development by asking students and teachers alike to pay attention to how the study of biology, for example, means not only learning a body of knowledge but also learning how to do things with others—formulate problems, design research, and evaluate the significance of results. Teachers have two important tasks in group work: to design tasks that develop group work skills and to provide a level of support commensurate with the new challenge of group work.

References

Bennis, W. G., and Shepard, H. A. "A Theory of Group Development." *Human Relations,* 1956, 9, 415–457.

Goodwin, L., Miller, J. E., and Cheetham, R. D. "Teaching Freshmen to Think: Does Active Learning Work?" *BioScience,* 1991, 41, 719–722.

Gordon, G., and Morse, E. "Creative Potential and Organizational Structure." *Journal of the Academy of Management,* Spring 1969, pp. 37–49.

Gordon, T. *P. E. T.: Parent Effectiveness Training.* New York: Penguin, 1975.

Hirsh, S. K., and Kummerov, J. M. *Introduction to Type in Organizations* (2nd ed.). Palo Alto, Calif.: Consulting Psychologists Press, 1990.

McCormick, K. "The Worcester Sixth Grade S-STS Evaluation Studies: An Overview." Paper presented at the 7th Annual Technological Literacy Conference, Alexandria, Va., February 7, 1992.

Mednick, S. "The Associative Basis of the Creative Process." In S. Mednick and M. Mednick (eds.), *Research in Personality.* New York: Holt, Rinehart, & Winston, 1963.

Michaelson, L. "Small Groups: A Potential Solution to the Problems of Large Classes." Paper presented at the 12th Annual Lilly Conference on College Teaching, Oxford, Ohio, November 20–22, 1992.

Miller, J. E., and Cheetham, R. D. "Teaching Freshmen to Think: Active Learning in Introductory Biology." *BioScience,* 1990, 40, 388–391.

Myers, I. B. *Introduction to Type.* (rev. ed.) Palo Alto, Calif.: Consulting Psychologists Press, 1991. (Originally published in 1962.)

Slavin, R. E. "Cooperative Learning." *Review of Educational Research,* 1980, 50, 315–342.

Sharan, S. *Cooperative Learning in the Classroom: Research in Desegregated Schools.* Hillsdale, N.J.: Erlbaum, 1984

JUDITH E. MILLER is associate professor of biology and biotechnology at Worcester Polytechnic Institute in Worcester, Massachusetts.

JOHN TRIMBUR is associate professor of English at Worcester Polytechnic Institute.

JOHN M. WILKES is associate professor of sociology at Worcester Polytechnic Institute.

This chapter considers the relation between collaborative learning and some major theoretical and empirical approaches to the fostering of critical thinking.

Critical Thinking and Collaborative Learning

Craig E. Nelson

The power of collaborative learning to enhance liberal and professional education is often underutilized, even in courses in which collaborative activities predominate. And students sometimes find collaborative activities engaging but not transformative. A coupling of collaborative learning with critical thinking can transform education much more effectively than the pursuit of either alone.

This chapter provides an introduction to key aspects of the pedagogy of critical thinking and their relationships with collaborative learning. It should enable practitioners already familiar with either approach to move quickly to incorporate a combination of the two approaches into their teaching. The examples have been chosen to illustrate the power of such a combined approach.

Enabling students to think critically is one of the central objectives of liberal and professional education. That students find this objective challenging is often quite puzzling to faculty. It would seem that a quick demonstration of a more powerful way of thinking should be sufficient for any intelligent student and that a little practice could be in order. This is rarely the case. Thus, it is apposite to ask, Why are critical thinking skills so hard for students to acquire?—a variant of the larger question, Why is it so hard to help students learn anything but facts and ideas that they can treat as facts?

It is much harder to foster real learning than one would imagine. For example, most students who pass traditional physics courses actually retain their prior, typically pre-Newtonian, views of reality (Arons, 1990). That is, although they learn to solve the problems, they do not understand the fundamental concepts of the course.

NEW DIRECTIONS FOR TEACHING AND LEARNING, no. 59, Fall 1994 © Jossey-Bass Publishers

The responses of faculty to such difficulties are often counterproductive. When our teaching is not working as well as we like, we often prepare the content more intensively and grade more leniently. When this combination fails to produce enthusiastic classes and good ratings—and fail it predictably does—we often conclude that our students are dumb, lazy, or hopelessly ill prepared (Boice, 1992).

The three frameworks developed in this chapter—mental models, discourse communities, and collaborative learning and discipline communities—propose answers to the question, Why do our students not think more critically about our disciplines? (Kurfiss, 1989, has a more intensive literature review.) These answers lead to solutions that are much more helpful than the conclusion that something is incurably wrong with our students. Collaborative learning is a key part of every solution. Indeed, for many students, the acquisition of critical thinking skills may actually require collaborative learning. A focus on critical thinking can make collaboration more effective and interesting for all students.

Mental Models: Knowing Wrong Things Interferes

Let us return to physics. Suppose that I toss a ball into the air, catch it, and then ask students what forces act on the ball halfway up. Only about 10 percent of the students in an introductory college physics course have entered the seventeenth century. These few Newtonians will answer that the only significant force is gravity, which acts to slow the ball's rise. The other students will give answers that reflect alternative, often tacit, non-Newtonian views of reality. One common answer is that the force of the hand is still acting on the ball. Much of the students' direct prior experience has been that, when one stops pushing something—for example, a desk across a carpet—it stops moving. Typical physics courses produce no significant change in the percentage of students who eschew such Aristotelian notions (Arons, 1990).

Stated in general terms, we each have in our mind explicit and tacit summarizations (models) of past experience, and we try to fit new experiences to our models (Piaget, 1967). Such behavior is actually quite reasonable: Often we have had extensive relevant experience. And even bright and hardworking students will change their models only if they see a clear conflict between those models and their experience. Even then, they must decide that the conflict is important enough to work through.

Tie a weight to a string, whirl it around your head, and let go, so that it hits a target. Most people who try this feel a weight pulling on the string, recall their experience with many other pulls, and predict that we should release the weight when it pulls straight at the target. So we may be surprised to see that, if we release the weight when it pulls straight at the target, it moves in a direction 90 degrees away from the target. That is, it continues in the direction in which it was moving, not in the direction in which it was pulling, at the time when it was released. The pull is the force required to deflect it from that straight path and keep it going in a circle. Once our original prediction is contradicted, a few of us will consider changing our minds, but most of us must experience additional contradictions. Between 70 and 90 percent of the members of a class will revise their models to agree with the current physical model after five or six nonredundant sequences of prediction and unexpected results (Arons, 1990).

An anecdote illustrates the implications. In conversation, a chemist noted that he was good at writing multiple-choice questions: He found it intuitively easy to construct alternative answers that students who did not quite understand the concept would prefer to the right answer. I congratulated him and then asked how he taught the students to avoid such wrong answers. There was a long pause, after which he replied: "That's not a bad idea!" As Arons (1990) notes, one of the most important things that we can learn from students is why they give incorrect responses to practice assessments. We can use these reasons to identify where the interpretations go astray and help the students learn to avoid the wrong answers.

Such behavior requires a radical change in our view of our responsibilities. In most disciplines, faculty have been responsible only for teaching the right way to view the material. The mental models approach makes us just as responsible for helping students to understand what is wrong with alternative interpretations. Otherwise, any hard work that they do, such as by studying, is more likely to make misinterpretations permanent than it is to correct them.

What does this claim have to do with collaborative learning? There is simply not enough time for the faculty member alone to discover and work through all the misunderstandings. We can engage the students collaboratively in this enterprise in several ways. For example, consider a teach-write-discuss-process approach. At the end of each testable unit (maybe eight to twelve minutes in a freshman lecture), we can display a transparency showing a short essay question or a few multiple-choice questions over the unit just taught. The students write down their answers and a brief explanation of why their answer is good and then compare answers. This brief interaction will allow many misunderstandings to be corrected. After these brief collaborations, many students, primed by their small-group discussions, may be more willing to participate in whole-class discussion. Moreover, students typically regard it as fair for faculty to call on them to report what their pair concluded, whereas they often resist being called on in the absence of such interchanges. Either of these approaches or a poll of the class will find the array of answers that still seem reasonable and why, which shows us what misconceptions need to be addressed and what content needs to be taught or retaught.

Discourse Communities

A further explanation of why critical thinking is difficult to acquire emerges from an understanding of discourse communities (Bruffee, 1984). In most discourse communities, which are imbued with social traditions, great emphasis is given to such factors as deference to authority, unreflective intuition, social dexterity, and timely action (Sternberg, 1990). In contrast, in academia each of us is responsible for justifying our own beliefs and actions in ways grounded in reason, evidence, and the values that we affirm personally. One of the central challenges of college is the psychic disequilibrium attendant on the reorientation to past authorities—peers and parents—that academic discourse asks. In other words, it is no longer enough that my dad says so.

One might expect the challenges of reacculturation to be restricted to areas that the students feel to be controversial—for example, creationism or social roles. However, the challenge is both deeper and broader. Mathematics is said to be the universal language. It is not clear at first glance how one might teach it in a culturally biased way. Nevertheless, when Treisman and colleagues (Treisman, 1986; Fullilove and Treisman, 1990) began to examine calculus at the University of California at Berkeley, he found that about 60 percent of the rural whites and some ethnic minorities were making grades so low that they could not proceed with a major in mathematics, science, or technology. His attempts to find something wrong with these students that would account for their performance all failed. In the process, he noted that, for the members of these groups, higher math entry scores predicted lower achievement in calculus. That is, the more math the students already knew, the worse they were likely to do.

Treisman eventually found that students from these groups had certain experiences in common. They felt socially marginal at Berkeley. They tended to be from high schools that were not heavily oriented toward college preparation, and they thus had few peers with whom to study. Moreover, they had often been taught that only weak students studied together (as in remedial study halls) or even that working together on homework was cheating. Finally, in their high school peer communities, studying and academic achievement had had negative social prestige—they made you a nerd—so many of the students studied alone, virtually in secret. The greatest contrast was with Asian Americans, who had formed study squads to get through calculus. In these groups, social status was increased by an individual's ability to teach others.

Treisman's response focused on taking control of the social system. He invited the students from underrepresented groups to an honors discussion section. That is, he was very careful not to call it a remedial section. He told them that homework would be easy both because their math scores showed that they were ready for calculus and because the class would prepare them for it. However, the homework had to be submitted on time. In order to help them get it right, he required them to do peer checking. Required collaboration cut the time devoted in class to discussion of homework from the entire period to an average three minutes a week. During class, Treisman (Fullilove and Treisman, 1990) used collaborative small groups with harder problems. Note the shift to coaching. If you want students to run a hundred-yard dash, you do not let them stop at 100 yards. If you want them to do well on an exam at the level of the homework, you must lead them beyond the homework. He also organized group social activities on weekends so that members felt much less isolated and became more likely to collaborate informally.

As a result of the formalized and informal collaborations, the proportion of D, F, W, and I grades dropped from about 60 percent to about 4 percent, and the differences between the average grades achieved by rural white and African American students who did the investigator's "workshop" calculus and the average grades for students in socially dominant groups—urban whites and Asian Americans—vanished. Success with this approach has now been achieved at institutions very different from Berkeley and in physics, chemistry, and biology as well as in mathematics.

This example illustrates three key points. First, the reacculturation that college demands is not restricted to controversial topics but rather is part of all courses. Second, large increases in student success can be made by instituting structured collaboration and increasing opportunities for informal collaboration. Third, collaboration is important in achieving even the simplest form of critical thinking—complex correct thinking—where all students should get the same answer (here, to calculus problems).

Collaborative Learning and Disciplinary Discourse Communities

The differences between the communities that a student encounters before college and the general academic conversation in college are large and potentially overwhelming, but the problems do not end there. There are also large differences among individual disciplines. Although we often believe that we are teaching in plain English, disciples impose severe conventions, and these conventions differ markedly among disciplines.

Thus, the expected responses to structurally identical questions can differ radically among fields. Consider *Compare plants and animals* in biology and *Compare Hercules and Hamlet* in English. In biology, we expect the student to list five to ten important points. A student who applies the same approach to the question about Hercules and Hamlet ("both lived in ancient times") is in deep trouble. In humanities, a compare question should elicit one or two existentially important theses (say, the trade-offs in human affairs between action and reflection). However, the student who applies the humanities approach in biology class is also in trouble. While a miniessay on "the most interesting point of comparison between plants and animals—the power of movement" is certainly defensible, it is likely to omit several expected points, and the instructor is likely to give it a low mark.

Disciplinary expectations extend well beyond essay exams. The same book can be assigned in two or more disciplines, and it must be read differently in each. Students need to be taught the kinds of questions that a discipline asks of texts. All writing tasks carry marked discipline-based expectations. Critical thinking is governed by conventions that define what counts as evidence, what criteria to apply, and whether to focus on internal or external reality as well as many other considerations.

Another example may help. Williams (1990) notes that one of the hardest things about learning to write in a discipline is figuring out what one cannot say or use as evidence. Tacit conventions exclude many accurate statements. While an observation like *The color of the pH indicator exactly matched the central stone in my grandma's garnet brooch* may be very accurate, it is usually unacceptable in a science class. Similarly, explaining Shakespeare's references to the "jeweled eyes" of toads by retinal structure is not considered a positive addition to most analyses of his plays. Further, in struggling to master the forms of discourse, students often make many errors in grammar and writing mechanics that disappear spontaneously as soon as they have mastered the conventions (Colomb, 1988). Thus, the differences in disciplinary expectations are so severe that, even if they know and understand the material, bright, hardworking students can do poorly on many assignments and exams.

What can we do? A colleague facing these problems found that she could make her students brighter and harder working in one hour of class time. She provided sample essay questions and an array of answers and asked the students to decide collaboratively in small groups which answers were which good and which were not. She also asked them to decide what made answers good or bad, and she made sure that they saw the key differences. Once the students understood the conventions associated with the discipline (and with academia in general), their essay answers improved remarkably—not only in that course but in other courses as well.

My colleague's efforts illustrate two key insights for teaching that flow from the recognition of disciplinary discourse conventions (Bruffee, 1984). First, it is helpful—necessary really—to try to make the tacit disciplinary expectations explicit. In my experience, simply naming the conventions is not sufficient. It helps to give students specific guidance in seeing and using the expectations: for example, study questions for reading assignments, detailed structure and guidelines for writing assignments. One major difficulty in making disciplinary conventions explicit is that faculty themselves often were not taught the conventions explicitly but learned them by doing. Often, we do not notice when we have stopped talking plain English. Thus, it may not be easy for us to articulate our mastery of our discipline's conventions. Another is that our own expertise can mask many details of the process for us. If we do something often enough, many of the steps involved become so routine that we are no longer conscious of performing them. These difficulties mean that we need to learn or relearn the problems that the novice encounters. The mental models approach helps here.

Robert Grossman (personal communication) has found that exam grades for students from discussion sections led by advanced undergraduates were higher than those for students from sections led by faculty. I suggest that the reason is that advanced undergraduates had clearer recollections than faculty of the challenges in learning the discourse peculiar to the discipline.

The second insight flows from the exercise of having students collaborate to discover the criteria for judging essay answers. Collaborative work is very effective in helping students to understand and master a discipline's conventions. In the past, much of this collaboration took place outside the classroom, but we can teach much more effectively and fairly by incorporating collaboration explicitly into the central activities of our courses. And making a discussion of the conventions an explicit part of the conversation will make the collaboration more effective.

Moreover, if we contrast the expectations of our discipline with those of other disciplines, we provide a higher-level framework (mental model) for thinking reflexively about thinking, a core critical thinking skill (Perry, 1970). For example, we can teach students collaboratively or to ask questions about the applicability of a variety of disciplines to a real-world situation (Paul, 1990). We can also provide these frameworks by comparing alternative paradigms. Bleich (1978) has students examine several critical theories and then collaborate to develop their own approaches to literary analysis. Grossman (in press) has students collaboratively examine the same psychological case with four different analytical frameworks.

Despite the power of the mental models framework and the disciplinary discourse framework, especially when the two are taken in conjunction, a third approach is also important. It shows why efforts to teach critical reasoning and sophisticated discourse often fail even when we work with the students' prior mental models, provide them explicit models of disciplinary reasoning, and use extensive collaboration.

Intellectual Development

An even deeper difficulty for the learning of critical thinking skills comes from our unchecked expectation that students have already developed the intellectual capacity needed to understand the way in which our disciplines work. It is helpful to distinguish several capacities that we want students to master. One includes such basic right-answer reasoning skills as the use of syllogisms, the ability to understand area and volume in terms of unit squares and cubes, and an understanding (not just an ability to execute) mathematical operations. I term this level *complex-correct thinking*. Arons (1990) lists the general and quantitative reasoning skills associated with this level.

Piaget (1967) provides a framework that explains many of the problems delineated by Arons (1990) and others. Children initially acquire skills in concrete tasks, and only with more experience and maturation do they become capable of dealing with ideas and reasoning operations in the abstract, that is, as formal operations. Understanding mathematical equations without needing to think of specific concrete examples and understanding the concept of a tragic hero rather than just picturing particular heroes are two examples of formal operations. In many institutions, a majority of the entering freshmen are not yet ready for courses based on formal operations, but many first-year courses require them. For example, Herron (1975) lists sixteen competencies integral to freshman chemistry that appear to require formal reasoning. Arons (1990) provides extensive examples of how we can help students to master complex-correct formal reasoning tasks.

However, even students who are fully competent at formal operations may still not be capable of many of the tasks that faculty usually characterize as critical thinking. I have asked more than three thousand faculty participants in workshops to envision the critical thinking skills that they would like to teach. Well over 90 percent of the tasks that they have specified require understanding beyond the right-answer focus of basic formal operations. Perry's (1970, 1981) scheme of intellectual development helps us to understand some of the central tasks that students face after they become capable of formal operations. That scheme can be simplified to four different approaches to intellectual challenges.

Dualism is the simplest approach. It divides reality into polar categories, such as good and bad or true and false. Students who use this approach expect to learn either things that they can memorize or the right way to find the one true answer (complex-correct thinking). They can do well in courses that focus on recall or on problems with unambiguous right answers. They often regard the role of faculty as one of emphasizing the parts of the text that they are to memorize.

Our primary teaching task with such students is to show them the extent and scope of legitimate uncertainty in the areas that we teach. No one can think critically about things that seem unquestionably true. However, these students are so resistant to uncertainty that they may suspect a teacher's competence if they are shown two ways of working a problem. Nelson (1989) discusses some general approaches to delineating the uncertainty in one's field.

When students see that there is no guaranteed right answer in an area, their typical response is to conclude that all opinions in the area must be equally valid. Lacking any better standard, they pick an opinion because it feels intuitively okay, much as one picks a flavor of ice cream. Perry (1970, 1981) termed this stage *multiplicity*. For most graduates of four-year programs, multiplicity is the most sophisticated mode that they use spontaneously in thinking about real problems. In this sense, liberal and professional education generally fail even for most of the students whom we graduate.

The transition from dualism to multiplicity requires students to recognize that uncertainty is inevitable on many questions. The transition from multiplicity to increased sophistication requires students to recognize that, despite this uncertainty, we can still often select one or more ideas or productions (be they poems, scientific theories, or nursing plans) that are superior to most other productions of the same type. As an alternative, we recognize that, although there is a fair range of acceptable productions, many others are demonstrably terrible. Our primary teaching task becomes one of showing how we recognize acceptable, better, and terrible within our discipline.

When we claim that one theory is better than others, two questions immediately arise: What are the alternatives? And what are the criteria that justify this judgment? Students can think more critically if we explicitly delineate both the alternatives and the criteria that we use to adjudicate among them (Nelson, 1986, 1989). Thus, when I teach evolution, my goal is not belief. Rather, my task is to help students master the criteria used in science to judge which theories are better (Nelson, 1986).

As students learn to use criteria, they begin to treat intellectual activity as a game, either the teacher's game or the discipline's game. They view such activity as a game in two senses. First, there are good and bad moves, and students learn to tell the right moves from the rules of the class or the discipline. Second, students have the choice of playing or not playing. There is a strong element of sophistry: Instead of the notion that all opinions are equally good, which characterizes multiplicity, students now often still think privately that all frameworks are equally good but that within a disciplinary framework one can tell better from worse and otherwise proceed to make sense of the chaos of uncertainty. This stage can be described as *contextual relativism*.

The necessity for further development can be seen if we examine the development of empathy (Belenky, Clinchy, Goldberger, and Tarule, 1986; Perry, 1970). When we treat issues as dualists, we rely on an authority to provide the answers. We do not ask why authority chose them; it seems clear that authority chose them because they are the truth. Since we do not understand why our group believes as it does, we have no base for understanding why other groups believe differently—they are simply wrong. Indeed, we often regard other views as not just factually but also morally wrong—as evil (Perry, 1970). Thus, we have no base for either intellectual tolerance or empathy.

In areas that we treat with multiplicity, we believe that authority cannot provide dependable answers. If we must pick an answer, we do so unreflectively. Thus, we have no articulated understanding of our choice and hence no grounds for intellectual empathy. But we want others to tolerate our choices, and thus we expect to tolerate theirs. This position leads us to try for unlimited tolerance in areas where we see that there are no clear answers.

In the intellectual games of contextual relativism, we understand that people living in different contexts often legitimately have different beliefs. We may even make one of our central tasks understanding how intelligent, even brilliant people past and present ever came to believe things so different from what we currently believe (Russell, 1945). We are thus rapidly developing the capacity for intellectual empathy. But we still have unlimited tolerance for different frameworks of belief. Great tolerance might seem to be a virtue, but students here often carry it to extremes. Given an introduction to modern German history, they can see that Hitler was brilliant and effective in many ways. But they are reluctant to say that key parts of what he did were wrong or crazy (Belenky, Clinchy, Goldberger, and Tarule, 1986).

To make such judgments, we have to assert our own values as preferable. We have to begin to take stands again, as we once did in dualism, but our enterprise is based now on an articulation of our own values and analyses, not on an echo of authority's positions. To do this, we must adjudicate among various combinations in different contexts. Thinking becomes more complex. We come to see knowledge as constructed rather than discovered, as contextual, as based inevitably on approximations, as involving trade-offs in values, and as requiring us to take stands and seek actively to make the world a better place (Belenky, Clinchy, Goldberger, and Tarule, 1986).

When we as faculty fail to get students to this level of critical thinking, we leave them poorly prepared to deal with personal and professional decisions and with the major issues of our times. Diversity, social problems, environmental issues, and the changing geopolitical system all require minds that can grapple successfully with uncertainty, complexity, and conflicting perspectives and still take stands that are both based on evidence, analysis, and compassion and deeply centered in values. This ability must be a major goal of liberal and professional education.

Collaborative Learning and Intellectual Development

Intellectual development is the most elaborate of the schemes that I have presented for the fostering of critical thinking. It is also the one that has been most helpful to me in understanding how to use collaborative learning effectively in college classes. For collaborative learning to be most effective in fostering critical thinking, it is not sufficient simply to have students work together. Undergraduates typically relate to most tasks with a mixture of dualism and multiplicity. Left alone, they often simply create a collage of opinions. We need to provide students with an intellectual scaffolding that helps them approach their tasks in ways more sophisticated than those they would use spontaneously.

In terms of the models discussed here, such scaffolding can be provided in three ways: as models or frameworks that allow students to think about their thinking; as alternative possibilities within disciplinary discourse; or as an introduction to uncertainty, with alternatives to be compared and criteria for comparing them. Indeed, the collaborative task can focus explicitly on the utilization of any one of these approaches. Without such scaffolding, collaboration seems more likely to make the students' current modes of thinking permanent than to stimulate sophisticated thinking.

The collaborations that I find most effective in fostering the more sophisticated kinds of critical thinking (those besides dualism and multiplicity) are structured by teachers and executed by students. They encompass three key steps: preparation, cognitive structuring, and role structuring. Preparation can be achieved either by structuring a shared background or by selecting for discussion points on which all students can safely be presumed to have some relevant knowledge. A common background can be provided by readings or other assignments outside class; by experiential learning, including labs; or by presentations in class. Common background can be assumed for a question like, What have you heard to be the problems with evolution? By *cognitive structuring,* I mean providing students with questions or analytical frameworks that are more sophisticated than those that most would have used spontaneously at the beginning of the semester. The question, What assumptions underlie this argument? serves this function for many classes. Role structuring is the specification of a collaborative process that is sufficient to get all the members of a group to participate meaningfully and to minimize behaviors that inhibit group progress.

For example, consider the teach-write-discuss-process exercise discussed earlier. The lecture segment and the writing time prepare the students for collaboration. An appropriate question provides cognitive structuring: It prompts students to more sophisticated thinking than would come spontaneously. Finally, working briefly in pairs on something that each student has written provides enough role structuring that most students participate actively and fairly evenly.

My second example illustrates increased role structuring. First, have the class read an assignment and write out answers to some open-ended questions that are more sophisticated than those that most students would ask spontaneously of themselves. Regardless of whether the reading and writing are done before or during class, the questions provide both preparation and cognitive structuring. In "round-robin" format, students present their answers and discuss their reactions. Each student in turn gets to continue until formally announcing "I've finished." Then each student notes the positive things that he or she has gained from collaborators, again ending with "I've finished." Thereafter the collaboration is unstructured.

This technique produces unusually effective communication. In less structured modes, if I have a new idea and pause to get it straight, someone else starts talking. If, in contrast, I suddenly realize how the material at hand sheds light on some aspect of my own life and pause to decide whether to share, someone else usually starts talking. Moreover, in unstructured exchanges, we often put more energy into thinking about what we are going to say next than we do into listening. Thus, this approach fosters careful listening, increases participants' freedom to develop ideas, and clarifies statements of consequences and values. Each of these results appreciably enhances our ability to foster critical thinking.

My third example illustrates increased cognitive structuring, and it is thus especially relevant to intellectual development. I often have the students in a class fill out a worksheet before collaborating. A typical worksheet asks the student to identify the author's main points, the support that the author offers for each point, an evaluation of the strength of that support, and the burden of proof that the student advocates for each point. Burden of proof involves a choice between the skepticism of the scientist who rejects a point until it has been shown to be probably true and the alternative, which accepts a point until it has been shown to be probably false. The student must justify his or her choice by explicitly stating the consequences on which the student bases the choice and the strength of evidence that would cause the student to reverse his or her current position. This approach takes uncertainty and adjudication as foundational and further asks students to justify their choices in terms of consequences and competing values. Nelson (1986, 1989) offers examples. This approach thus uses cognitive structuring to elicit higher-order critical thinking. Students who complete the worksheet before class are clearly well prepared. In class, I ask them to use ink of a color that contrasts strongly with the ink used in preparation. This lets me assess extent of preparation simply by scanning the papers. Role structuring is provided in part by making participation a group task. This method attempts to elicit thinking that goes well beyond dualism and multiplicity and places disciplinary games in a larger framework.

The effective fostering of higher-order thinking brings us back to reacculturation. The development of higher-order critical thinking must of necessity change our relationships to past authorities. A woman in her late twenties remarked near the end of my evolution course, "I finally understand why this course has been so hard for me—it is the first time I have ever thought differently from my mother, and it has been very hard on both of us." Undergraduates often decide explicitly not to think critically about religion (Perry, 1970). For many families, adopting a different religion would be an explicit, often unforgivable, renunciation of family identity. As we attempt to foster critical thinking, we must remember that we are asking students to make appreciable changes in their identity.

It seems to me that, as we become more sophisticated, we switch from an identity based on what one believes and does—an identity base that persists from dualism through contextual relativism—to an identity based instead on conscious choices as we choose what to believe and do—a sense that our processes for choosing are likely to be more persistent than many of the choices that we have made. In so doing, we redefine our social universe (Loevinger, 1980).

Whether we view these changes as intellectual development or reacculturation, the existential challenges are great—so great that, when we try to think in new ways, we may feel crazy or bad. Our thoughts may feel okay only when we enunciate them to our peers and our peers accept them. Moreover, striving for peer approval may be one of the more important motivations for thinking thoughts different from those of our mother and other members of our nonacademic communities of discourse. Listening to my classes and examining their papers suggests that most students do by far their most serious rethinking of their views during and in preparation for collaborative sessions. Collaboration thus often provides the most effective stimulus for the changes required for greater sophistication. Simultaneously, it provides the social support needed to make those changes emotionally acceptable.

Conclusion

Let us return to the question, Why do students do poorly in our courses? In this chapter, we have considered some alternative perspectives that help us, instead of wishing that students were not dumb, lazy, or ill prepared, to teach the students whom we actually have. Students often have explicit or tacit models of reality and analytical tasks that make it difficult for them to do well. We can expand our teaching to discover these models and help students see what is wrong with them. Students often have not understood what we expect in general academic or specific disciplinary discourse. We can provide explicit introductions to the conventions of individual disciplines and take responsibility for building structured, collaborative student discourse communities. Finally, the students' general expectations of knowing often differ from our own. In particular, we expect an acknowledgement of the extent and sources of uncertainty, the use of criteria to adjudicate among possible formulations, and, often, the judicious assertion of values as part of the grounds for choice and action. We can teach these features explicitly and provide the support that will enable students to reorient their relationships with other authority figures. With each approach, structured collaborations increase the number of students with whom we will be effective. And these approaches will in turn increase both the effectiveness of our uses of collaborative learning and the enthusiasm with which the students embrace them.

References

Arons, A. B. *A Guide to Introductory Physics Teaching*. New York: Wiley, 1990.

Belenky, M. F., Clinchy, B. M., Goldberger, N. R., and Tarule, J. R. *Women's Ways of Knowing*. New York: Basic Books, 1986.

Bleich, D. *Subjective Criticism*. Baltimore, Md.: Johns Hopkins University Press, 1978.

Boice, R. *The New Faculty Member: Supporting and Fostering Professional Development*. San Francisco: Jossey-Bass, 1992.

Bruffee, K. "Collaborative Learning and the 'Conversation of Mankind.'" *College English*, 1984, *46* (7), 635–652.

Colomb, G. G. *Disciplinary Secrets and the Apprentice Writer*. Upper Montclair, N.Y.: Institute for Critical Thinking, Montclair State College, 1988.

Fullilove, R. E., and Treisman, P. U. "Mathematics Achievement Among African American Undergraduates of the University of California Berkeley: An Evaluation of the Mathematics Workshop Program." *Journal of Negro Education*, 1990, *59* (3), 463–478.

Grossman, R. W. "Encouraging Critical Thinking Using the Case Study Method." *Journal on Excellence in College Teaching*, in press.

Herron, J. D. "Piaget for Chemists." *Journal of Chemical Education,* 1975, 52 (3), 146–150.

Kurfiss, J. *Critical Thinking: Theory, Practice and Possibilities.* Washington, D.C.: Association for the Study of Higher Education, ERIC Clearinghouse, 1989.

Loevinger, J. *Ego Development: Conceptions and Theories.* San Francisco: Jossey-Bass, 1980.

Nelson, C. E. "Creation, Evolution, or Both? A Multiple Model Approach." In R. W. Hanson (ed.), *Science and Creation.* New York: Macmillan, 1986.

Nelson, C. E. "Skewered on the Unicorn's Horn: The Illusion of [A] Tragic Trade-off Between Content and Critical Thinking in the Teaching of Science." In L. W. Crow (ed.), *Enhancing Critical Thinking in the Sciences.* Washington, D.C.: Society for College Science Teachers, 1989.

Paul, R. W. *Critical Thinking: What Every Person Needs to Survive in a Rapidly Changing World.* Rohnert Park, Calif.: Center for Critical Thinking and Moral Critique, Sonoma State University, 1990.

Perry, W. G., Jr. *Forms of Intellectual and Ethical Development in the College Years: A Scheme.* New York: Holt, Rinehart & Winston, 1970.

Perry, W. G., Jr. "Cognitive and Ethical Growth: The Making of Meaning." In A. W. Chickering (ed.), *The Modern American College: Responding to the New Realities of Diverse Students and a Changing Society.* San Francisco: Jossey-Bass, 1981.

Piaget, J. *Six Psychological Studies.* New York: Vintage, 1967.

Russell, B. *A History of Western Philosophy.* New York: Simon & Schuster, 1945.

Sternberg, R. J. "Thinking Styles: Keys to Understanding Students." *Phi Delta Kappan,* January 1990, pp. 366–371.

Treisman, U. "A Study of the Mathematics Performance of Black Students at the University of California, Berkeley" (Doctoral dissertation, University of California, Berkeley, 1986). *Dissertation Abstracts International,* 1986, 47, 1641A.

Williams, J. M. *Style: Toward Clarity and Grace.* University of Chicago Press, 1990.

CRAIG E. NELSON is professor of biology and of public and environmental affairs at Indiana University.

This chapter focuses on the current and future use of technology in collaborative learning classrooms with practical reference to group decision support systems, electronic classrooms, interactive video, and hypermedia systems.

Computer Technology and Collaborative Learning

Patricia Sullivan

Why have teachers found it challenging to structure collaborative learning in electronic classrooms? This chapter answers that question, examining the difficulties in the use of collaborative strategies with many of the ways in which computers are currently used for instruction. Focusing on the experiences of teachers of writing, the author discusses the adjustments that teachers need to make as they decide to use collaborative strategies in electronic classrooms. The expression *electronic classroom* is sometimes applied to distance education classes that use computers. In this chapter, it refers to a class taught in a classroom equipped with networked computers.

Three premises underlie this discussion. First, computer support for collaborative learning in college (particularly when the subject is writing) should have collaborative learning, not individual learning, as the goal. Second, the transfer of pedagogy from traditional to electronic or computer classrooms requires complex adjustments and substantial rethinking of the ways in which classroom time is spent. Third, because computer support for collaborative learning is relatively new, it often provides tools for collaboration. but it does not always provide an integrated environment for the use of those tools.

Current work shows the necessity for computer support of collaborative efforts in a variety of curriculum areas (Koschmann, 1992). This chapter concentrates on writing instruction and shows how college teachers struggle to bring collaborative learning to fruition in computer classrooms. Writing is one area in which traditional classrooms have made extensive use of collaborative pedagogy. This heritage is an impetus to the application of collaborative pedagogy to the teaching of writing in electronic classrooms.

NEW DIRECTIONS FOR TEACHING AND LEARNING, no. 59, Fall 1994 © Jossey-Bass Publishers

There are several reasons why writing instruction is a good proving ground for the collaborative use of computers. Writing is a question more of mastering a set of skills than it is of controlling a body of knowledge. And while it is born out of a print culture that fosters the notion of single authorship, it has been widely accepted that most practical writing—that is, most of the writing done in the workplace—is performed collaboratively or cooperatively. Writing instruction that focuses on collaboration in many ways contests the publishing process enshrined in the traditional print culture.

Computer environments for the teaching of writing, which until recently were equivalent to word processing rooms, often include a variety of software and networking capabilities. Thus, computers and writing instruction can be used more fully in group-based learning.

To examine the problems that teachers have when they try to use collaborative learning in electronic classrooms, this chapter looks at the views underpinning the development of software for computer-based education and for collaborative work. Through a review of computer support for writing instruction, the article argues that software designed to aid in collaborative learning originates from conceptualizations of group learning, while more traditional software and hardware originates from traditions of individual learning.

Traditional Models of Computer Support for Instruction

There are three broad categories that describe the ways in which educational software has been used in traditional computer-based education: drill and practice, such as tutorial programs, instructional games, and simulation (Alessi and Trollip, 1985); computer tools, such as word processors, data base management systems, spreadsheets, and graphics programs (Dede, 1988); and instructional activities, such as computer programming and computer literacy.

Makrakis (1988) combines views of the computer as a device for individualized instruction and as a medium of interaction into eight modes of delivery and interaction: drill and practice, tutorial, instructional games, simulation, problem solving, spreadsheet, word processing and data base management.

It is the interest in interaction that opens the traditional models to the kinds of software needed to support collaborative learning. Even discussions of computer-assisted instruction—often viewed as covering only drill and practice and tutorials—value interaction. For example, Steinberg (1990) defines computer-assisted instruction as individualized, interactive, and designed to limit a student's incorrect learning.

Clearly, interactive learning is being embraced both by people who see it as opening up computer-based instruction to student-led discovery or investigation (such as in multimedia and hypermedia programs) and by people who see interactive learning as a way of making computer programs more interesting to students. But the interaction that these people imagine is one-on-one dialogue between student and computer, dialogue in the service of individualized learning.

In writing instruction at the college level, computers have most often been centered on word processing. The college uses of computers tend to fit into the open-ended modes that Makrakis (1988) identifies. In the area of computers and writing, only a few people have developed classifications of computer uses, perhaps because the teachers involved saw themselves as writing teachers rather than as developers of computer-based education.

Discussions of categories focus on classifications of uses and objectives (Schwartz, 1982; Burns, 1987), empirical results of the use of word processors to improve writing (Hawisher, 1989), and critiques of the categories proposed (Ohmann, 1985; Kaplan, 1991; Hawisher and Selfe, 1990). The journal *Computers and Composition* devoted a recent issue to software (LeBlanc, 1992). A bibliography in that issue (Strickland, 1992) divided forty-six entries by use: to help writers collaborate over a network (six); to help writers invent (eight); to allow comment after critical reading (five); to help writers write research papers (eight); to help writers analyze style, mechanics, and usage; to offer reference guides on-line (five); to author multimedia courseware (six); and to help assess writers (one). Clearly, collaboration has a place in the current classification of software uses for writing instruction. In the bibliography just mentioned, it is linked to networking. Elsewhere in the same issue, collaboration was linked either with networking or with hypermedia.

Computers and Collaboration in Writing Instruction

Five scenarios illustrate some of the potential and some of the problems that writing instructors face when they attempt to couple computers with collaboration in writing instruction.

Scenario 1. A group of three must confer about a project that they are developing together. However, they cannot all make an evening meeting in the computer lab. Two come in and work on the document in their class folder and save it to the teacher's folder for comments. Later, the person who could not meet comes into the lab to review the changes that her colleagues have made, but she cannot access work stored in the teacher's folder.

Scenario 2. To save system space, the members of a writing class are directed to post their mail to a campus computer bulletin board rather than to use e-mail. The teacher makes an initial posting that asks students to discuss the student newspaper. By the next day, the teacher's posting has attracted several vicious responses from people on campus who are not in the class. Students are mystified and refuse to write to the computer bulletin board.

Scenario 3. Students are asked to read a hypertext novel in StorySpace[1] and build a class reading by annotating the document and then passing it on. Some students remember to use a special font to highlight their contributions, but other students add to the text in the font that the author has used. After the entire class has read the text, they compare it with the original to begin to build an understanding of collective reading habits.

Scenario 4. The teacher asks the class to use Interchange[2] conferencing software, which allows class members to share their writing in real time, to discuss the assigned reading. For some reason, most of the students have not read the material and cannot write about it, so they chat. The teacher unsuccessfully tries various strategies to get them on task in developing a collective reading of the article. Frustrated that the students have not taken the task seriously, the teacher prints the transcripts and makes each person write a critique of the reading with only the transcripts as evidence.

Scenario 5. A class relying on peer critique moves into a computer classroom and uses Prep Editor[3], which enables students to make their comments alongside the text. Writers find this style of comment more compelling during revision, and the teacher notes that different types of comments are made and that more care is given to what is said.

Scenarios 1 and 2 highlight some of the potential and some of the problems associated with the use of computers on networks. In scenario 1, the computer's accessibility accommodates the team, but because they do not understand how to manipulate files, a member of the student team is left out. In scenario 2, the campus bulletin board is too public a forum for classroom conversation, and the teacher and students do not realize it until too late. These two cases suggest the transfer of pedagogy from traditional to computer classroom is not a simple matter. All aspects of student and teacher actions need to be reconsidered when a class moves from a traditional to an electronic environment.

Scenarios 3, 4, and 5 illustrate three pieces of software that can be used to promote collaboration in the writing classroom, although they can also produce problems of their own. Scenario 3 demonstrates the potential of hypertext as a tool for teaching collaborative and critical reading, but it also shows that users need a clear understanding of the tools at hand. Scenario 4 shows that use of a technology that in principle seems to give everyone in class equal say can backfire in certain situations. The frustrated teacher's response to the problem reinforces authority structures in the class—perhaps quite the opposite of the original intent. Scenario 5 discusses the potential effects of moving peer critique from a set of comments made on discrete sheets of paper in a traditional classroom to the placement of an intertext of commentary alongside the text critiqued in an electronic classroom. The proximity of the intertext to the actual text keeps the comments current during revision and provides visible cues that an intertext of response has been created.

The Challenges of Teaching Collaboration in an Electronic Writing Classroom

Connections between collaboration and pedagogy are normally mediated by instructional theories. For example, in writing instruction, collaboration was widely discussed in the 1970s and 1980s from several perspectives. At the beginning, it was embraced as a way of helping teachers to deal with under-prepared students and of tapping the power of peer learning without changing what students learned (Bruffee, 1984). Social constructionists, arguing that all knowledge is socially constructed, embraced collaboration as a pedagogy of choice because it acknowledges multiple authorship (Trimbur, 1989). Feminists embraced it because, they felt, it better reflects women's ways of knowing (Belenky, Clinchy, Goldberger, and Tarule, 1986). Technical, business, and professional writers also embraced collaboration as a component of writing because research on writing in the workplace had shown that collaboration is central to workplace communication (Ede and Lunsford, 1990; Sullivan, 1992). In all these pedagogies, *collaboration* has held at least two meanings. Sometimes, it stands for writing produced by a group. At other times, it describes the teaching of writing through peer responses and critiques. Collaboration has been praised by many groups for different reasons.

Introduction of computers into the picture further complicates the issue. Some proponents of collaboration oppose the use of computers on political and theoretical grounds (Ohmann, 1985). Others, who under different circumstances would have sympathized with those who resist technology, describe computers as naturally inviting collaboration and joint authorship (Gerrard, 1991). These people often suspect that those who teach English will object to computer use.

Further, it is apparent that advocates of computer use in collaboration (issues of *Computers and Composition* often have an article that deals with collaboration) do not hold a unified instructional theory. Hence, the pedagogical advice that new teachers seeking guidance about the use of collaboration in electronic classrooms find may not match their own theories. Under such circumstances, it takes time and confidence to sort out the various meanings of collaboration in electronic settings.

Space and Time in Electronic Classrooms

In electronic classrooms for writing instruction, each student usually has a microcomputer that is connected to a network in the classroom or a wider area. As a rule, all the computers are located in the same room. We are beginning to have experience with electronic classes in which the computers are located in many different rooms and connected via network. These classrooms add layers of complexity to this discussion (Moran, 1992).

This physical arrangement reinforces students' isolation, even when the computers are grouped. So, a student can resist participating in an oral discussion by playing with her or his own interactive television or by participating in competing conversations on the network. The teacher is no longer the clear physical center of the class, a point that leads many to claim that electronic classrooms promote student-centered curricula. But certainly the psychological space of the classroom is altered.

If the collaborating group uses the computer as a medium for an electronic meeting of the minds, as do participants in on-line conferences and users of computer bulletin boards and e-mail, physical isolation can be combated in several ways. Network users can be asked to discuss a topic in groups until they reach consensus. They can be asked to research opinions by searching out appropriate bulletin boards and querying users. Or they can exchange sections of documents for evaluation or hold an on-line class discussion. If class discussions are held on-line or even if some class time is devoted to writing, it soon becomes clear that the time spent actually drafting text goes up dramatically in an electronic classroom. Barker and Kemp (1990) argue that networked classrooms cope with the deterrents to group work that are found in traditional classes—poor physical environment and domination of the class by a few class members. But electronic classrooms may pose physical problems that are just as profound, and opening a classroom to participation does not ensure that everyone will in fact participate.

If classroom activities focus on the use of word processing software to produce texts, collaboration becomes much more tricky. In such situations, we need methods for sharing texts as they are developed and revised, and we need to teach these methods to students. Moreover, they may disrupt the habits that students have established for composing text. It may be inviting to move to such programs as Prep Editor, which was mentioned in scenario 5. Other programs help with the invention and revision of text (Strickland, 1992). But these programs have to be researched, acquired, evaluated, learned, taught, and integrated into the curriculum. Integrating such programs with other software can be troublesome. For example, it can prove difficult to transfer text to a commercial page layout program. The teacher quickly faces a dilemma: Is the easy sharing worth the investment of time and resources?

New teachers often embrace word processing software because they know it. In the mid 1980s, word processing software was heralded as a boon to the teaching of writing. After all, it could make many of the complex processes involved in writing observable. Years of study have cast a doubtful light on claims that such software increases fluency or facilitates revision (Hawisher, 1989). Still, new teachers of writing who enter an electronic classroom are most likely to know word processing software and to turn to it first. Thus, their base software was developed for use by a single author as a publishing tool. True, the new word processing programs are quite flexible. For example, Microsoft Word includes many layout features, a simple drawing package, a spelling checker, a voice annotator, and a thesaurus. The output of such programs can also be easily imported into other kinds of programs. For example, it is now possible to embed a chart in a document so that the chart is updated whenever the spreadsheet to which it has been linked is updated. But such programs are only beginning to support group collaboration, and these commercial products will be oriented toward the needs of business, not of teaching. Meanwhile, the teacher has to figure out how to make word processing software support collaboration in the classroom.

The Investment and Risk of New Technology

Scenarios 3, 4, and 5 demonstrated three collaborative activities: a joint reading, an on-line conference, and group annotation of a single text. These activities demonstrate the use of collaborative tools. Happily, a number of tools are available for collaborative writing instruction. Strickland (1992) lists eight that are appropriate for and aimed at college writing.

However, tools alone do not overcome the difficulties of using collaboration in writing classes. Unless and until an environment or a set of coordinated environments supports the full range of collaborative activities that students and teachers need to perform in an electronic classroom, the task of the teacher who seeks software to support collaboration will be fragmented. That teacher will need to work hard to locate programs and find resources that can be used to fund evaluation for local use. She also will have to evaluate how new programs create problems in the use of existing programs. She must also find funds to purchase what is needed and adjust the curriculum so that these new resources can be used. If students are required to learn programs that they do not think they will ever use again and if the programs are difficult to learn, students are likely to resist using them. The teacher must then decide how much class time can be devoted to the learning of new software.

Conclusion

This chapter has argued that collaboration can be supported by computers in electronic classrooms but that teachers who want to use computer-based education should be aware that traditional educational software was developed to facilitate individual learning. Writing instruction illustrates this point.

Computers can work to strengthen collaborative learning of writing. But they require work on the part of teachers: work to build curriculum, create new purposes for current software, seek out alternative software, learn that software, and fit it into the curriculum.

The easy solution in the electronic writing classroom—a focus on word processing—favors individual instruction. While a number of software products are being developed to assist collaboration in writing classes, each product tends to handle one type of activity important to the class. This way of solving the problem means that schools will invest considerable sums of money in the software and that teacher and students will have to invest considerable time and effort in learning to use it. The interest that the commercial sector has shown in building computer support for collaborative work is encouraging. As products develop that include collaborative activities in a collaborative environment, the ability to use computers for collaborative learning and work will expand. Writing teachers can look forward to computer support that allows students to collaborate more easily. But commercial word processing software dominates computer-based instruction in writing. The commercial packages were developed for office work, not for instruction, and it is likely that the coming collaborative environments for writing will also be developed for office work without much input about collaborative writing processes from writing teachers. That gap will continue to drive the development of educational software.

Notes

1. StorySpace (Eastgate Systems, P.O. Box 1307, Cambridge, MA 02238) is a hypertext program for the Macintosh environment that allows students to create hypertext documents (LeBlanc, 1992).
2. Interchange (The Daedalus Group, 1160 Clayton Lane, Suite 248-W. Austin, TX 78723) is a component of the Daedalus Integrated Writing Environment that offers real-time conferencing to facilitate on-line discussion. Two windows are used—one for composing messages and one for reading the messages that scroll across the screen.
   Scenario 4 shows that synchronous conferences can be used in negative ways. Most of the literature on conferencing packages is very positive about their power to facilitate class discussions. Such packages as Interchange and Real-Time Writer 2.0 (Real-Time Learning Systems, 2700 Connecticut Avenue N.W., Washington, DC 20008–5330) are available for both Macintosh and DOS systems. For Macintoshes only, there are Aspects (Group Technologies, 1408 N. Fillmore Street, Suite 10, Arlington, VA 22201), Conference Writer, and Live Writer (RDA/Mind Builders, 10 Boulevard Avenue, Greenlawn, NY 11740). Strickland (1992) has more information about these tools.
3. Prep Editor, a prototype software product under development at Carnegie Mellon University (e-mail: prepproject@andrew.cmu.edu), allows coauthors and commenters to put marginal comments in columns adjacent to the text (Strickland, 1992).

References

Alessi, S. M., and Trollip, S. R. *Computer-Based Instruction: Methods and Development.* Englewood Cliffs, N.J.: Prentice Hall, 1985.
Barker, T. T., and Kemp, F.O. "Network Theory: A Postmodern Pedagogy for the Writing Classroom." In Carolyn Handa (ed.), *Computers and Community.* Portsmouth, N.H.: Boynton-Cook, 1990.
Belenky, M. F., Clinchy, B. M., Goldberger, N. R., and Tarule, J. M. *Women's Ways of Knowing: The Development of Self, Voice, and Mind.* New York: Basic Books, 1986.
Bruffee, K. A. "Collaborative Learning and the Conversation of Mankind." *College English,* 1984, *46,* 635–652.
Burns, H. "Computers and Composition." In G. Tate (ed.), *Teaching Composition: Twelve Bibliographic Essays.* Fort Worth: Texas Christian University Press, 1987.
Dede, C. J. "Empowering Environments, Hypermedia, and Microworlds." In T. R. Cannings and S. W. Brown (eds.), *Update to the Information Age Classroom.* Irvine, Calif.: Franklin, Beedle & Associates, 1988.
Ede, L., and Lunsford, A. *Singular Texts, Plural Authors: Perspectives on Collaborative Writing.* Carbondale: Southern Illinois University Press, 1990.

Gerrard, L. "Computers and Compositionists: A View from the Floating Bottom." *Computers and Composition,* 1991, *8* (2), 5–15.

Hawisher, G. "Research and Recommendations for Computers and Composition." In G. E. Hawisher and C. L. Selfe (eds.), *Critical Perspectives on Computers and Composition Instruction.* New York: Teachers College Press, 1989.

Hawisher, G. E., and Selfe, C. L. "The Rhetoric of Technology in the Electronic Writing Class." *College Composition and Communication,* 1990, *42* (1) 55–65.

Kaplan, N. "Ideology, Technology, and the Future of Writing Instruction." In G. E. Hawisher and C. L. Selfe (eds.), *Evolving Perspectives on Computers and Composition Studies.* Urbana, Ill.: National Council of Teachers of English, 1991.

Koschmann, T. (ed.). *SIGCUE Outlook,* 1992, *21* (3) (entire issue).

LeBlanc, P. (ed.). *Computers and Composition,* 1992, *10* (1) (entire issue).

Makrakis, V. *Computers in School Education: The Cases of Sweden and Greece.* Stockholm: Institute of International Education, University of Stockholm, 1988.

Moran, C. "Computers and the Writing Classroom: A Look into the Future." In G. E. Hawisher and P. LeBlanc (eds.) *Reimagining Computers and Composition: Teaching and Research in the Virtual Age.* Portsmouth, N.H.: Boynton-Cook, 1992.

Ohmann, R. "Literacy, Technology, and Monopoly Capital." *College English,* 1985, *47* (7), 675–689.

Schwartz, H. J. "Monsters and Mentors: Computer Applications for Humanistic Education." *College English,* 1982, *44* (2), 141–152.

Steinberg, Esther. *Computer-Assisted Instruction.* Hillsdale, N.J.: Lawrence Erlbaum, 1990.

Strickland, J. "An Annotated Bibliography of Representative Software for Writers." *Computers and Composition,* 1992, *10* (1), 25–35.

Sullivan, Patricia. "Computer Classrooms and the Collaborative Education of Professional Writers." *SIGCUE Outlook,* 1992, *21* (3), 55–58.

Trimbur, John. "Consensus and Difference in Collaborative Learning." *College English,* 1989, *51* (10), 602–616.

PATRICIA SULLIVAN is associate professor of English at Purdue University.

This chapter explores how instructors can effectively evaluate the development of students' knowledge acquisition and skill in collaborative settings.

Assessing Effectiveness in the Collaborative Classroom

Sharon Farago Cramer

When a faculty member considers implementing a collaborative classroom, what issues regarding assessment need to be considered? Imagine the following situations:

E., a second-year faculty member, read the first six chapters of this book and started to change all her courses for the coming semester. She excitedly discusses her ideas with colleagues, but she becomes increasingly disenchanted with each conversation. In answer to the question, How will you grade your students fairly? she tightens her lips, shakes her head, and sighs. She does not know what to do, so she decides to forget all about it.

D., a tenured full professor, used the first six chapters of this book to adapt one of his courses. However, he did not change his grading policies. Instead, he graded as he always had. So when students ask him how he plans to grade their group participation, he is embarrassed. He is unsure how to respond, since he is not exactly sure himself. He realizes that he should have read the chapter on assessing students before the semester started.

K., the department chairperson, is reviewing faculty evaluations at the end of the semester. Half of the students in a course with a strong collaborative component were ecstatic about it, while the others felt that the teacher had gotten away with murder by having based their grades in part on the collaborative work that they had done with each other.

The author thanks Sharon Raimondi and Richard Towne, State University of New York College at Buffalo, for their helpful comments during the revision of this chapter.

Introduction

Colleges rely on faculty to evaluate students' knowledge fairly and effectively at the end of every course. In typical courses, this evaluation is relatively easy to do. Different types of formative and summative evaluations—for example, pop quizzes, midterms, finals, essay examinations, research papers—are generally sufficient to lead to a final grade. However, in collaborative learning, as Slavin (1990) has cautioned, both group goals and individual accountability are essential for student achievement. This can pose problems for the instructor.

This chapter helps faculty by defining assessment, describing various classroom learning environments in which collaboration can take place, and proposing guidelines for grading when collaborative learning is used. Faculty must help students to understand how their collaborative learning results in end-of-semester grades. The criteria for success that the faculty member has developed must be stated in the course syllabus, just as they are in courses taught in the traditional manner. However, ongoing formative assessment enables the instructor and the students to keep track of progress throughout the semester. Meaningful assessment, which enables both instructor and students to monitor progress, should be an ongoing, continuous process rather than linked only to final grades.

Definitions

This chapter is based on the following view of assessment: "Assessment is typically associated with the possession of information rather than [with] the mastery of ongoing processes (like learning to write, revise, and take criticism or, even more radically, to integrate the results of a critique into a work) . . . If assessment is to be a moment in an educational process rather than simply an evaluative vehicle, then it must be seen as an opportunity to develop complex understandings" (Zessoules and Gardner, 1991, p. 51).

Assessment is part of the process of learning, and it engages both teacher and student. Assessment, in other words, must provide multiple opportunities for the measurement of mastery associated with processes and yield data that an instructor can use to develop a course grade. To meet these two goals, two types of assessment are integral to the collaborative college classroom at both the undergraduate and the graduate levels: assessment during process and assessment of product.

Assessment During Process. Periodic collection of work, such as drafts, journals, reflections, and progress reports, can help to determine students' current status in particular projects. Some of the material collected will not require direct feedback but instead be checked off as a progress report. The value is in the process of the work itself. Other collected work may receive formative commentary, oral or written, before the project is completed for formal grading.

Howell, Fox, and Morehead (1993, p. 87) describe the benefits of gathering ongoing information on student progress: "Because learning is indicated by a change in behavior across time, it can be seen in the progress of a student toward a performance objective. This is formative information, and it is important because progress data are uniquely suited to deciding how to teach. Progress data tell you where the student is and, more important, where she is going. This type of data is fluid, or dynamic, showing both the direction and [the] magnitude of change."

Assessment of Product. One kind of assessment focuses on a student's accomplishments and mastery in the course or on a project. Students can receive assessment as individuals for group work or a grade for the entire group project.

When a combination of approaches is used throughout the semester, graded assessment becomes woven into the fabric of the course.

The goal of grading is accurate measurement of the knowledge that students accumulate in the college classroom. To achieve this goal in the collaborative classroom, students and instructor attend to the differences between passive and active learning. Both students and instructor must become increasingly knowledgeable about the assessment process. The active involvement of students in assessment enables them to become more thoroughly engaged in the learning process, which transforms the learning experience (Cramer, 1990).

Both assessment during process and assessment of product are discussed in the context of the learning environment descriptions provided later. These different learning environments illustrate the changes that take place over the course of the semester with students at different points in the collaborative process. This discussion clarifies how the assessment schema designed by the instructor must match the type of collaboration taking place in the classroom.

Learning Environments

To illustrate the various approaches that can be used in the collaborative classroom, I will use a model of learning environments based on Hersey and Blanchard's situational leadership model (Hersey and Blanchard, 1982; Hersey, 1984). Under that model, we can distinguish four kinds of classrooms, differentiated on two characteristics: task and relationship. As the authors of the chapters in this sourcebook make clear, students in a collaborative classroom start by being passive learners and end up becoming accountable for their own learning. They eventually are weaned from dependence on the instructor for feedback and become increasingly able to foster their own successful learning.

These descriptions are independent of the disciplines taught in classrooms. Although the ultimate goal of a collaborative classroom is to move from low to high levels of student effectance—Boucher and Weinstein (1985, p. 130) define *effectance* as "doing something by oneself with the things in one's environment"—every classroom does not necessarily manifest all four approaches. Individual instructors need to select the point at which they plan to start the class and the point at which they want to end and work toward increased collaboration among students in the class.

Environment I: High Task, Low Relationship. In a classroom characterized by a high task, low relationship environment, students receive directions for a collaborative group activity from the instructor and carry it out with minimal modification. The instructor does little in the way of relationship building to motivate students to solve problems on their own. For example, a chemistry instructor gives six examples of acceptable experiments to be conducted during the next scheduled lab session. Collaborating students select and perform one of the experiments exactly as presented.

Environment II: High Task, High Relationship. In a high task, high relationship environment, the instructor not only gives students directions for group academic tasks but also gives them guidance and support. Improving students' skills and motivating them to collaborate are joint objectives. For example, an instructor teaching an introductory course on public speaking can design a computer simulation that students can use when critiquing a panel presentation. Its prompts can include task-related ideas (for example, constructive criticism) as well as supportive comments.

Environment III: Low Task, High Relationship. In a low task, high relationship environment, students work more independently and use a collaborative approach successfully. The instructor provides intermittent input and correction, but students are able to work well most of the time on their own. For example, in the final third of an advanced counseling course, an instructor assigns a group of collaborating students to design and conduct a panel interview with a potential client. The instructor gives input only as needed.

Environment IV: Low Task, Low Relationship. Students are autonomous and take primary responsibility for designing and carrying out their own learning. For example, collaborative student groups in an undergraduate introductory retailing course develop procedures for conducting an end-of-year inventory. Student groups seek specific feedback from the instructor, but they do not rely on the instructor for direction. By taking ownership of their learning process, students "become independent, collaborative, and cohesive" (Boucher and Weinstein, 1985, p. 135).

Discussion. The four learning environments just described give instructors options in terms of overall goals for student participation in collaborative activities. A variety of assessment mechanisms are required in these settings. In a relatively traditional classroom, the grading assessment approach alone can usually suffice. However, a combination of formative and summative approaches adapted to the environment of the particular classroom can help both instructors and students throughout the semester. The remainder of this chapter shows how approaches with and without feedback to students can be used in conjunction with grading in the collaborative classroom.

Assessment Process

Various monitoring techniques are described in this section. An advantage of these techniques is that they do not require the same amount of time spent in formal grading, yet they still provide both instructors and students opportunities for appraisal. The techniques can be used weekly, in several of the environments described above, and include six different approaches: a strategy to quickly anticipate or "look back" on the class activities, student self-monitoring activities, anonymous evaluations, reactions to student papers, and collaborative group activities.

Class Assessment. At the start or end of class or at both points, the instructor can ask pointed questions, the answers to which can be used to take the pulse of the class. The instructor can use the answers to these questions to determine which learning environment characterizes the class and how homogeneous the students are. The following questions can be posted or shown on an overhead at the start of class: What grade would you give yourself right now for your preparation for class? What grade would you give yourself right now for your readiness to contribute to your collaborative group? In the last week, how many hours did you invest in work related to this course? What do you most want to learn about during today's class? If you could give your collaborative group one sentence of advice to improve your work together today, what would it be?

The following questions can be posted or shown on an overhead at the end of class: What grade would you give yourself for the effort that you put into today's class? What grade would you give your collaborative group for its productivity today? What grade would you give your collaborative group for cooperation and effective problem solving today? What percentage of what you learned with your collaborative group today was new to you? What percentage of what you learned from the lecture today was new to you? Did you learn what you thought you would most like to learn during today's session? If you could give one sentence of advice to the instructor about what could have been done to improve today's class, what would it be?

This procedure for monitoring students can enable those who work and think quickly to respond easily. If some students seem to be frustrated by time constraints, use chart paper to post the end-of-class questions at the beginning of the session.

Checklists. Checklists are one useful tool for student self-monitoring. Checklists can be distributed to students before collaborative learning activities begin. They can be particularly helpful for students in the high task, low relationship environment, where students need direction from the instructor. Figure 7.1 shows a typical checklist.

Checklists can prompt students to look for specific contributions that they make to the group (for example, *Volunteers appropriately when tasks need to be accomplished*) as well as provide information about how students evaluate

Figure 7.1 Checklist for Collaborative Learning

Learning Environment I

Directions: Using a scale from 1 to 5, in which 1 means that you demonstrate the skill consistently, 3 that you demonstrate the skill occasionally, and 5 that you need improvement in use of the skill, rate yourself on each of the following items.

_____ Incorporated prior knowledge into classroom discussions
_____ Asked questions of group members in an open-minded way
_____ Built on comments of other group members to enhance discussion
_____ Volunteered ideas in a constructive manner
_____ Helped the group to summarize its progress
_____ Identified missing information in the group plan
_____ Built on ideas from others

themselves. Checklists can be completed anonymously, and group results can be compiled and presented to the class in table form. Depending on the learning stage of the class, the instructor can provide more or less guidance. In a high task, low relationship environment, the instructor presents a model for students to replicate. In a high task, high relationship environment, the instructor can use the questions as a checklist. In a low task, low relationship environment, students can independently generate alternatives themselves with indications of the strengths and weaknesses of each approach; in this envirnoment the more autonomous students are capable of both developing and evaluating options without the kind of supervision that students in a high task environment require.

Journals. Students can maintain personal journals around topics pertinent to the course. Figure 7.2 shows an outline that can help students to organize their journal entries.

As Drews (1972, p. 224) points out, student self-study and self-evaluations "nearly always include false starts." Making substantive comments on thirty to fifty journals could pose a problem for the instructor. Instead of deciding not to have students keep journals or having students keep journals but feeling guilty about never checking them, instructors can use journals in various ways throughout the semester. For example, journals can be a means for students to focus on self-monitoring. Instructors' feedback becomes less central, and instructors' review can focus on self-reflective comments that appear in the journals (Surbeck, Han, and Moyer, 1991).

Another approach is a progress report without personalized feedback in which assessment is less focused on student self-monitoring. For example, journals can be collected either at random or on assigned dates, reviewed, and returned to students. The instructor can comment in general terms about concerns raised in the journals on particular topics and set up collaborative

Figure 7.2 Journal Monitoring

Learning Environment I

Purpose: This outline provides guidance in formulating comments for your journal entries.

I. Reaction (to class material, small-group activities, and so on)
   A. Positive feelings
   B. Negative feelings
   C. Report
   D. Personal concern
   E. Issues
II. Elaboration (on any of the preceding topics)
   A. Concrete elaboration
   B. Comparative elaboration
   C. Generalized elaboration
III. Contemplation
   A. Personal focus
   B. Professional focus
   C. Social and ethical focus

Source: Surbeck, Han, and Moyer, 1991.

groups in response. For example, students in a Spanish literature course with a high task, high relationship environment can be asked to respond in their journals to the following instruction: *In this week's reading assignment, list the major cultural and political problems faced by the main characters.* The instructor, when returning to the journals, can post a frequency chart that shows how often individual problems were mentioned. Such a chart enables students to get feedback with minimal effort on the part of the instructor.

The instructor can then form collaborative groups to discuss key problems identified by the majority. As an alternative, the groups can address the problems that only a few students identified. These groups can help the instructor to address issues of cohesiveness and accountability that are key to effective collaborative groups (Furtwengler, 1992).

The instructor can support students who attempt to work through problems in their groups unsuccessfully. As Svinicki (1992, p. 1) explains, "learning, like all other creative acts, will flourish in an atmosphere in which the learner is willing to take risks, and it is the task of the instructor to create such an atmosphere for learning." Self-evaluation is an essential feature of the collaborative classroom (Slavin, 1991).

Anonymous Group Member Evaluations. The instructor can take primary responsibility for the development of anonymous group member evaluations. In a high task, low relationship classroom, such evaluation takes place throughout the semester, while in other types of classrooms, students can

Figure 7.3 Group Member Evaluation Form

Learning Environment III

Class member being evaluated

Overall rating scale: 1 (low) to 5 (high) _____

Demonstration of professionalism with regard to team project

_____ Prompt in attendance at team meetings

_____ Complete in delivering agreed-upon parts of project

_____ Organized in seeking information from resources (other team members, instructor, library)

_____ Volunteers appropriately during team meetings when tasks need to be accomplished

_____ Pulls fair share with regard to overall work load on project

Demonstration of initiative with regard to project

_____ Develops ideas constructively with others

_____ Makes helpful suggestions on ways of accomplishing projects

_____ Is a good listener

_____ Seeks input from quieter team members

_____ Includes ideas from others when summarizing

Demonstration of effectiveness in independent work

_____ Selects a project topic and makes necessary modifications without undue fuss

_____ Meets deadlines

_____ Demonstrates knowledge of the topic selected for the project

_____ Shares resources as appropriate

_____ Incorporates materials presented in the course and outside the course into the project

Overall comments:

What specific suggestion would you make to this individual for work on future group projects?

What was the individual's most valuable contribution to the group?

modify evaluations over the course of the semester. A low task, high relationship classroom can be given the project of developing a group evaluation form. Figure 7.3 shows a group member evaluation form that the author developed and used periodically in a graduate research class.

Student Papers. Almost all student papers in early drafts can be submitted for review before they are formally graded. By providing various contexts for student practice efforts along with feedback, instructors can encourage higher-order cognitive strategies (Rosenshine and Heister, 1992). Limiting products to a certain number of pages—for example, two pages for an outline—can also reduce the time that the instructor spends on feedback.

Some papers can be designed specifically for the collaborative classroom, since this type of classroom structure enables students to reflect jointly on their experiences within the context of the discipline. Discipline-related theories presented in class or learned through independent research assignments can be applied to relevant collaborative classroom activities. For example, students in a political science class discussing the steps involved in translating legislation into regulations can identify ways in which their collaborative groups parallel those steps. Such an experience responds to Slavin's (1991, p. 42) recommendation that collaborative groups experience "periodic and regular group processing," because it means that students must apply content-related material to their own experiences in order to analyze their collaborative process.

Evaluating Collaborative Groups. If written analysis of collaborative groups is congruent with course goals, it can be incorporated into the course requirements, and a percentage of the course credit received can be based on it. For example, students can be made responsible for writing up the ways in which their collaborative group helped them to troubleshoot the difficulties that they encountered. Such a requirement would be very appropriate in the high task, low relationship or the high task, high relationship environment. A more advanced assignment appropriate for the low task, high relationship or the low task, low relationship environment is to require students to generalize the type of help received to future situations related to course content.

Johnson, Johnson, Holubec, and Roy (1988, p. 34) identify various expected group behaviors that can be used in collaborative classrooms: "Have each member explain how to get the answer . . . Ask each member to relate what is being learned to previous learning . . . Check to make sure everyone in the group understands the material and agrees with the answers the group has developed . . . Encourage everyone to participate . . . Listen accurately to what all group members are saying . . . Encourage each member to be persuaded by the logic of the answers proposed, not by group pressure; majority rule does not promote learning . . . Criticize ideas, not people." Instructors can use these behaviors as springboards for the written analysis. The same behaviors can serve as the focus for other relevant activities throughout the semester.

Assessment of Product

All instructors in collaborative classrooms must eventually decide the extent to which students' final grades will be interdependent. This section presents six approaches—student papers, research projects, short-answer exam questions, formative feedback on collaborative projects, collaborative exams, and collaborative assignments—ranging in focus from independent grades to interdependent grades.

Student Papers. Under the student papers approach, students do collaborative work and receive individual grades. At specified points in the semester, students write short research or reaction papers that address a content-related problem related to the course discipline. Outlines discussed in collaborative groups can result in papers that are graded individually. One part of the paper can include relevant personal experiences based on collaborative activities within the class. For example, in an introductory design course in which student groups analyze design features in various mediums, the personal section can be required to address ways in which the student can better understand the wide range of opinions about good and bad design and capitalize on them in future collaborative group work projects.

Research Projects. Under the research projects approach, students' work is collaborative, but grades are individual. In the course of the semester, students are often involved in research projects. Although they share resources and library work time or even brainstorm together, each student's final product, whether written, oral, or a combination of the two, is unique and graded individually. For example, in a language arts methods course for elementary teachers, students may have to research four different ways in which basic spelling can be taught and present the benefits and deficits of each approach. Using the collaborative groups in class, students can present both oral and written arguments for their choice at a simulated school board meeting. Students receive individual grades for their presentations and papers.

Short-Answer Examination Questions. Under the short-answer exam questions approach, students work individually, and they are graded individually. Since most of the learning expected in courses is content based, we can expect most evaluation measures to be based on students' understanding of course content. However, some instructors may choose to include several short-answer or multiple-choice questions on midterms and finals to evaluate students' understanding of course process as well as of content. These questions can be based on principles of collaborative learning or on the potential benefits of this approach in other situations (for example, negotiation, business development, student team teaching). This approach is in keeping with Marzano's (1992) suggestions for promoting self-learning in all aspects of the classroom.

Formative Feedback on Collaborative Group Products. Under the formative feedback approach, collaborative groups receive formative feedback during the semester on collaborative group products, and individual group members receive a summative grade on the group product at the end of the semester. The instructor can provide feedback to groups in a variety of ways. One strategy is to have groups submit their products electronically so that the instructor can include evaluative comments in their text. Chapter Six of this sourcebook reviews tools that support such a strategy.

Nonelectronic means, such as checklists or focused feedback (for example, review of lead sentences only), can limit the amount of time that the instructor spends on evaluation. The individual grade for the final product can be based on criteria announced in advance. These criteria can include those on which the formative evaluations were based.

Collaborative Examination. Under the collaborative examination approach, which is appropriate only in fully collaborative classrooms, the course syllabus gives students the option of collaborating during an examination and of accepting as individuals the grade that the group receives. While the option for individual work is almost always made available as an alternative, the instructor gives the students the option to choose to work together on some or all examinations.

Collaborative Assignments. Under the collaborative assignments approach, students are graded as groups. Work on a group paper or group research project can be very effective in a collaborative class setting. To increase the likelihood that all students do the work that has been agreed on, students write out and sign a contract for each section of the assignment. Students who do not complete their portion of the assignment do not receive credit for the assignment, and their final course grade reflects this lack of credit.

Group Grading Issues and Concerns

Most instructors use individual grading, and they are familiar with its costs and benefits. Because group grading may be new to many, this section discusses its pros and cons.

Many instructors who have used group grading agree on its visible benefits. It promotes active discussion and ensures personal responsibility for ongoing learning. Students come to joint testing sessions or group work sessions prepared. As one student put it, "I didn't want to look like an idiot to my group. I made sure that I knew the material—probably better than I did for exams when I had to study on my own."

Another benefit is the increased cohesion of groups in which members rely on each other for their final grades. The mutual goal can foster the kind of true collaboration that Boucher and Weinstein (1985, p. 135) describe: "Overall, the students in this course showed progress from dependency on authority to interdependency. Predictably, they pushed at the start of the course for instructor structuring, clarification, and expert opinion. Toward the middle of the course, they showed, predictably, ambivalence between wanting to be responsible and wanting authoritative guidance. And toward the end of the course, they became independent, collaborative, and cohesive within their groups, seeking instructor opinion and guidance minimally."

Two problems often arise with group grading: First, strong students carry weak students. Second, groups develop highly critical, competitive atmospheres. While these problems can occur even in traditional classrooms, their effects are particularly negative in collaborative classrooms. An instructor can use a variety of progress reports, some content based, others focused on group process, to become aware of problems and intervene. Another group-based approach, which should be included in the syllabus if it is used, is to give groups the option of putting a member on probation. In such cases, group members develop a contract for getting off probation. This contract has specific behavioral outcomes and sets deadlines. Failure to meet deadlines results in a predetermined consequence (for example, an additional independent study project or loss of a specific number of points).

For most instructors, a combination of individual grades and group grades can achieve the goals of collaboration without sacrificing individual accountability. Through the use of varied, ongoing assessment, instructors can monitor students' progress effectively throughout the semester regardless of the type of grading that they use. This tactic can work to the benefit of the instructor, the individual student, and the class as a whole.

Conclusion

Assessment of students in collaborative classrooms is ongoing, and it can be well suited to the particular needs of individual instructors. Because it is dynamic rather than static, assessment enables both instructor and students to reframe their personal understandings of the learning process and knowledge acquisition.

Overall, the challenges that a collaborative classroom poses to the college faculty member concerned about realistic assessment can be met through effective planning, careful consideration of course content goals, and student involvement. The outcome, more interactive than that in the traditional course, can enable both faculty and students to grow in unexpected, valued ways.

References

Boucher, C. R., and Weinstein, S. A. "Training Professionals to Be Powerful and Collaborative." *Contemporary Education,* 1985, *56,* 130–136.

Cramer, S. F. "Listening, Moving, Learning: Active Presentations for Large Classes." *Journal of Professional Studies,* 1990, *14,* 53–63.

Drews, E. M. *Learning Together: How to Foster Creativity, Self-Fulfillment, and Social Awareness in Today's Students and Teachers.* Englewood Cliffs, N.J.: Prentice Hall, 1972.

Furtwengler, C. B. "How to Observe Cooperative Learning Classrooms." *Educational Leadership,* 1992, *49,* 59–62.

Hersey, P., and Blanchard, K. H. *Management of Organizational Behavior: Utilizing Human Resources.* (4th ed.) Englewood Cliffs, N.J.: Prentice Hall, 1982.

Hersey, P. *The Situational Leader.* Escondido, Calif.: Center for Leadership Studies, 1984.

Howell, K. W., Fox, S. L., and Morehead, M. K. *Curriculum-Based Evaluation: Teaching and Decision Making.* (2nd ed.) Pacific Grove, Calif.: Brooks/Cole, 1993.

Johnson, D. W., Johnson, R. T., Holubec, E. J., and Roy, P. *Circles of Learning: Cooperation in the Classroom.* Alexandria, Va.: Association for Supervision and Curriculum Development, 1988.

Marzano, R. J. *A Different Kind of Classroom: Teaching with Dimensions of Learning.* Alexandria, Va.: Association for Supervision and Curriculum Development, 1992.

Rosenshine, B., and Heister, C. "The Use of Scaffolds for Teaching Higher-Level Cognitive Strategies." *Educational Leadership,* 1992, *49,* 26–33.

Slavin, R. E. *Cooperative Learning: Theory, Research, and Practice.* Englewood Cliffs, N.J.: Prentice Hall, 1990.

Slavin, R. E. *Student Team Learning: A Practical Guide to Cooperative Learning*. Washington, D.C.: National Education Association, 1991.

Surbeck, E., Han, E. P., and Moyer, J. E. "Assessing Reflective Responses in Journals." *Educational Leadership*, 1991, *48*, 25–27.

Svinicki, M. "If Learning Involves Risk Taking, Teaching Involves Trust Building." *Options: Faculty and Staff Development Advisory Council*, 1992, 2, 1–2.

Zessoules, R., and Gardner, H. "Authentic Assessment: Beyond the Buzzword and into the Classroom." In V. Perrone (ed.), *Expanding Student Assessment*. Alexandria, Va.: Association for Supervision and Curriculum Development, 1991.

SHARON FARAGO CRAMER is assistant professor in the Exceptional Education Department at the State University of New York College at Buffalo and president of the New York State Federation of Chapters of the Council for Exceptional Children.

This chapter illustrates some applications of collaborative learning in college classrooms.

Case Studies

Allen Emerson, Jerry Phillips, Cathy Hunt,
Arlene Bowman Alexander

Case I: The Interdependent Developmental Mathematics Classroom

When I began to work with groups, I was a traditional mathematics teacher. I lectured, and students listened. I began to change not because I had read the studies on collaborative learning but because I was frustrated. I never found time to lecture on all the material that students needed for subsequent courses without overrunning their understanding. Moreover, after almost twenty years, I had exhausted every trick that I knew to overcome students' hatred of mathematics and their resentment at having to take a noncredit course that does not figure in the calculation of their grade point average. Students refused to engage mathematical problems, nor were they capable of conceptualizing or articulating mathematical ideas. Teaching collaboratively has enabled me to get through more material, and students have achieved a deeper understanding, worked harder, and enjoyed it.

Overview. I started simply by dividing the class into groups and having students work in class on problems together. But over several semesters, I found that class dynamics required more than simple learning groups. I settled on four additional components: a text generated jointly by students and teacher, student learning logs, a teacher's log, and minilectures.

Student- and Teacher-Generated Text. I began my first group venture with the same text that I had used when I restricted myself to lecturing. Almost immediately two problems surfaced. First, some of the problems were too hard to work in groups. The difficulty was that the text forced students into an almost mindless repetition of problems that they had solved quite easily, because they worked so well in groups. In order to reduce the frustration, boredom, and socializing that emerged among groups, I found myself writing problems on the spot to supplement or replace those in the text. I suppose that the problems in the text had posed the same difficulties when I was lecturing and assigning homework problems, but now I was immediately aware of them, and I could do something about them.

Second, I could not shake the feeling that there was something about the nature of group work that set it at loggerheads with standard texts, however exquisitely organized and crystal clear they might be. From the students' viewpoint, the textbook interfered with their learning. From my viewpoint, it helped me to make efficient use of class time. Why was the textbook such a problem? My tentative answer is this: In the group learning context that I describe here, students solve problems first. Explanations come whenever necessary, either during the process or after. The reverse is true with a text: Authors expect students to read the explanations first and then solve the problems. The difference is between *I need to know now* and *Let me tell you everything that you will need to know before you begin.* When I tried to give the kind of explanation that a text would, I found myself lapsing back into the standard lecture method. And students began to nod.

As a result, we did not use the textbook much, so there was no point in having one. Instead, I write three or four problems on the board, even word problems, some of which I have prepared beforehand, some of which I improvise on the spot. Students copy them and work on them in their groups, asking for my help when needed. Each group writes its answers on the board. The other students and I then comment on the answers, and the group defends or amends its solutions.

Student Learning Logs. In the last five minutes or so of each period, students write responses in their learning logs to three standing questions and to one question that I change from class to class, depending on what I need to know. These are the three standing questions: What did you do today? How are the groups working for you? and Is there anything I should know about? Here is a typical question of the day: Was it a good idea to send helpers around, or should I stop doing this?

I collect the learning logs every period, read them, and respond to the students' comments. My replies range from a check mark or a brief phrase to a page or more of comment or the working out of the solution to a particular problem. The time that I spend responding to a single class for one period ranges from twenty minutes to more than an hour. Forty minutes is probably the average.

Several studies about writing in the mathematics classroom attest to its affective and cognitive value for students. Learning logs also tell me what problems we need to include in the text. Of course, I can see what is going on in the groups, but that is not enough. So for the question, How are the groups working for you? I often substitute these: Are you being ignored? Are you getting your questions answered satisfactorily? Is your group going too fast? Do you feel you are being put down?

Student Learning Groups. As I worked with groups, I could not decide on any fixed policy about if or when to change them. Most students did not want to change groups very often. A review of my teaching logs shows that I usually change groups twice a semester. Every semester, I have made accommodations for certain individuals, somehow to everyone's satisfaction, but it is a delicate matter to which I give some thought and care.

The groups range in size from three to five, but four students per group seems to be the most satisfactory. Students take tests individually, and I do not take any combination of group and individual effort into account when I compute grades. I do, however, give a retake for one examination and use students who have done well as helpers, raising their grades and giving them the day off on the day of the retake exam.

I do not assign roles—for example, moderator, encourager—but on several occasions I have suggested how the groups might work together on certain problems, for example, by agreeing on the first step, making sure that everybody gets through it, checking the intermediate results, ironing out discrepancies, agreeing on the next step, and so forth. Three times during the semester, I model the process by controlling the groups' progression through a problem. Student comments in response to my question, Was stepping through the group work helpful, or was it a waste of time? have been unanimously favorable.

Teacher's Log. In contrast to preparation for a traditional lecture, where I do all my development beforehand, I write in my teacher's log before, during, and after class. This practice became a necessity for me from the time I began using a teacher- and student-generated text. In the log, I write problems for the text before class, notes for any minilectures (some prepared, some spontaneous), and any problems written during class. The teacher's log, then, is my own counterpart to the student's log—my record of what I am learning about each class that I teach.

Minilectures. A minilecture serves two purposes: to introduce new material and to help students over the rough spots that they encounter. The minilecture is more compressed and highly charged than it is comprehensive or fully explanatory; it is more contextual than anticipatory of what is to come, more responsive to current problems than premeditated, and more improvised than highly content structured.

Results. As I said at the outset, I am able now to cover more material of greater difficulty without overrunning the students than I could with traditional lectures, at least if students' daily responses can be trusted. I have substantial evidence that students find the method engaging and that their attitudes toward mathematics have changed considerably. In four semesters involving more than 240 students, only five students said that they would have preferred the lecture method. The ability of students to conceptualize and articulate mathematical ideas increases as the course progresses, and their techniques are at least as well developed as they are under the lecture method. In short, the interdependent classroom does indeed do what I had hoped that it would, and my observations seem to be quite consistent with findings reported in the research literature on group learning.

Concerns. Nonetheless, I have some concerns. First, the main weakness of this method is that there is no supplementary material that students can work on outside class. This is not only my observation but also that of many students. Second, much of what we read in the literature about the benefits of group learning for students almost seems to glow, and so likewise do my student reports. But we do not read much about what it demands of the teacher, the amount of time that it takes, or how psychologically draining it is. My experience has been one of constant interest, stimulation, and watchfulness, but I always feel as if my classroom is hovering on the brink of pedagogical disaster. I never felt this way when I used the lecture method, perhaps because I felt that I owned the classroom. If a teacher is really aware of what is happening, teaching by groups is not a stable enterprise. It can veer rapidly from wonderful to terrible and back again at any moment. Third, I suspect that many of the courses that could be most effectively taught by group learning are often taught by the least senior people in the department, that is, by the people whose positions are most vulnerable to student evaluations. I do not mean to imply that group learning classes give me bad evaluations. Reading my students' journals would give the impression that I am terrific. Reading the institution's evaluation forms that the same students complete would give the impression that I'm mediocre to pretty good, depending on the class. There may be two reasons for this discrepancy. First, the institution's forms are designed specifically for the lecture method, as are the forms at many colleges and universities. Second, students may not make the connection between a positive experience in the classroom and the efficacy of the instructor, perhaps because the teacher's role is not what they are used to. The point is that use of the collaborative approach might result in bad to indifferent evaluations.

Nevertheless, the benefits of interdependence far outweigh the risks and problems. I would never return to the old days when I stood on one side of the classroom lecturing and students sat on the other side of the classroom listening.

Case II: A Collaborative Approach to the Teaching of Literacy Applications

Recently, I helped twenty-five graduate students to become more literacy proficient by examining with them their notions of literacy and its institutions. These students expected a traditional classroom lecture approach to learning: The teacher talks, the students take notes, and the teacher gives tests.

In this class, however, students explored ways of learning through a model based on the work of Wigginton (1987) and Ives (1987). The model uses tape-recorded oral interviews in a writers' workshop. To link the teaching of writing with reflective thinking through language interaction, this model suggests having students interview and tape-record the literacy life experiences of another person and keep a personal journal to record their own feelings about writing. The students selected individuals from the older adult community to interview. This approach allows the students to use language and social activity between two or more people to produce meaning (Blumer, 1969). The approach centers first on the students' lives, focuses then on the lives of respondents, and finally moves into the lives of other workshop participants.

Student- and Teacher-Generated Text. Thus, theoretically, I expected new writing perspectives to emerge from the interviews. I wanted students to control their writing. Therefore, I did not try to control how they managed their writing. Yet they demanded instruction and demonstrations, asked such questions as, Is this what you want? and made statements before the interviews signaling their fear of writing: "This writing stuff is hard work"; "I'm as good a writer as I want to be."

The students hesitated also to do oral interview work without demonstrations, and they were reluctant to interview informants without a preset package of interview questions. To negotiate their need for direction and my desire for noninvasive control, we grouped, brainstormed, and produced a list of collective questions from which students could choose to prime the interview that they conducted. Here are some of the questions: Where did you attend school? Tell me what going to school in those days was like. What are your favorite kinds of reading material? Who is your favorite writer? What time of day do you find most enjoyable for reading? If you were asked to write your memoirs, would you feel excitement or fear?

These questions gave the students a start. Other questions would probably emerge during the interview. Now they were on their own, first to gather information from the respondents, second to mold their data into a story, third to share and critique their story with fellow workshop participants, and fourth to produce a collaborative text of narratives.

Student Learning Groups. Using the oral interview as an instrument of learning, the students turned their findings into written narratives on literacy. During the workshop, the students shared their stories with others in collaborative learning/writing groups (Calkins, 1986).

Each student also read his or her writings aloud to another student and received feedback. This process was repeated at several editing sessions with students' writing collaborators and peers. One student recognized early on that everyone has problems but that no problem is so large that it cannot be overcome. "I feel great because I have a common problem with my classmates. Together we can work it out. I could not have handled this load by myself." Here, this student uses a gut response and a good use of strong feeling to evoke a strategy statement. The student's subsequent interview and written narrative attest to an execution of strategy and a way of grasping ownership.

Results. In this context, the students controlled their destiny by determining the social role of the workshop through the authority and direction that they themselves exerted. They negotiated what it all meant with other writers by sharing their writing. I allowed the students to do the work and decide the direction. When the students returned to the classroom with their rough drafts ready to share with co-writers, they took over the workshop. Yet I was available daily to receive and share their ways of learning.

The more students made decisions about what they were doing, the more motivated they became to continue their efforts, to write, and to search for their emerging writing voice. A journal reflection explains one student's attempt to internalize, project, and design the interview strategies: "I ask my peers if they are having trouble getting started on their interview. From all reports, they are not having much trouble. I guess it is just me. My problem is that I have too many other things on my mind. I need to relax and take one day at a time, stop worrying about the whole picture."

The last day of class, the students produced a final written narrative of the oral interviews and then bound individual personal copies in book form. One student shares her feelings about this transition: "Since I was a little girl, writing is something I always wanted to do, but I thought I never had the talent for it. Being able to write a story and see it in print is exciting." In these sentences, the student retrieves a feeling of joyous anticipation that she has missed for a long time. Clearly, she feels renewed, that all things are possible. The student used an awareness of a potential audience to shake up generative, critical, and expressive capabilities simultaneously and extend her own psychological growth through writing.

Concerns and Comments. First attempts are seldom successful. There is no magic formula. No experience in collaborative learning can be so structured as to be infallible. Any success to be had with collaborative grouping can be laid at the feet of past attempts.

If that learning takes place within social relationships, then many traditionalists will find collaborative grouping frustrating. Traditional assignments are easier for both teacher and students—perhaps because we resist change, but I suspect it is also because we do not know any different or because we lack courage.

Far too many students resist this nontraditional approach. These students do not know how to talk collectively, offer no suggestions, are not honest with each other, and are afraid of hurting each other's feelings. Thus, those wanting to hurry through, bent on treating their assignment like a traditional report, ignore any constructive criticism that they receive. I suspect they cannot grasp collaborative learning because they have little prior knowledge.

The role of the teacher under the collaborative approach frightens the students who are not used to it because it is far removed from the traditional role. An innovator's time and energy could be more productive if students did not expect all teachers to act the same.

Case III: Replacing Lecture with Collaborative Student Learning Activities in College Science Classrooms

The nine years in which I taught anatomy and physiology by the traditional lecture and laboratory method were measured as successful in many ways—by student achievement, student evaluations, and my own sense of accomplishment and exhilaration for a well-delivered lecture. Yet it began to dawn on me that I was the only one in the classroom who experienced such exhilaration. Moreover, I was becoming bored with the classroom experience and looking for new challenges. A semester when I taught only the lecture portion of the class was the last straw. I came to realize that, without the interaction that naturally occurred in lab, I hardly even knew the students. In fact, I rarely heard from them. It was then that I teamed up with Arlene Bowman Alexander, an instructor in human services whom I had seen facilitate a very dynamic student-centered classroom. Although our initial projects were not related to my anatomy and physiology classes, her philosophy and techniques began to spill over into them. She became my informal mentor, encouraging me to take risks and providing valuable feedback as I tried new approaches. Of course, I saw a major difference in her teaching task and mine: She had the luxury of those soft skill courses. I saw the primary question as one of learning how to remain content centered while being student directed. Together, we selected the model developed by Cross and Angelo (1988). Through a collaborative effort using focused listening, directed paraphrasing, half-sheet response, and other assessment techniques, students controlled and determined their own learning using the text, other readings, and video resources.

Activities. While the outcome of these techniques may appear to be fairly traditional, the approach that the class took to the activities was unique in three aspects: First, students complete learning activities in groups, not as individuals, whether in class or at home. Second, learning activities replace lecture. No comprehensive explanation is provided. Students discover content through their activities. Third, learning activities use the instructor to select learning resources, answer specific questions that arise from group discussion, summarize the activity, and provide feedback. The instructor is emphatically not a lecturer.

Each class session consisted of three components: an introduction aimed at motivating students and explaining class objectives; a collaborative student activity that asked participants to demonstrate some combination of understanding, analysis, synthesis, and evaluation of the resource content; and a concluding activity aimed at summarizing, reinforcing the learning, and connecting it with other learning in the unit.

Here is an example of the student activity: In teaching the topic of enzyme structure and function, I replaced the traditional hour lecture with a student group activity. Initially, group makeup was dictated by the classroom arrangement:

long, narrow rows of seats. Two students turned around in their seats to form a group with the two students behind them. I gave students specific directions and either a time or an item limit. At first, the questions were very general, for example, List all the important things that you can remember about enzymes from last night's reading assignment. Later, I instructed students to select the most important items, summarize them in narrative form, share their summaries with the class, identify unanswered questions, and connect their response to other class content. As the instructor, I became very instrumental in facilitating the last two processes.

The product of the student collaboration was either oral or written. When the product was oral, students, instructor, or both had an opportunity to provide feedback. The instructor evaluated written work and provided feedback to the group at the next class session. All group members shared any grade or points awarded equally.

Results. While the process just described was very stimulating for instructors, the bottom line is always, Did it work? To evaluate student achievement, we used the objective instruments that had been used in a comparable class the year before. We hoped to find that the student-directed collaborative approach to learning would give students the same mastery of content that they had achieved under the lecture method. That is, content would not be sacrificed by the limits of time or the absence of an authoritarian lecture. To our delight, stepwise multiple regression analysis revealed that the collaborative group activities accounted for an increase in test performance differences in American College Assessment Program score or age alone.

How receptive were students to this alternative learning design? More than half of the students thought that the activities were more interesting than those used in other methods and that they had helped them to learn the material better than other methods. Seventy-two percent thought the activities should be used in the next semester.

Student comments also suggest that students familiar with lecture as the primary means for delivering a large quantity of information from a highly qualified source may not be overly enthusiastic supporters of change that asks them to accept responsibility for learning and that asks them to become "experts." However, the majority of the students reported that they preferred the learning that they had accomplished in the collaborative groups to the cramming to which past experience had accustomed them.

The significance here is that not only have we found collaborative learning to be a sound instructional methodology but that high-content courses, such as the sciences, in which a vast amount of basic knowledge must be mastered, can be arenas for collaborative learning. This is exciting for those of us who teach the sciences and other high-content areas and find ourselves bored with lecture. Perhaps science lecture halls in the future will hear a significant amount of student talk.

Concerns. We have found that the most significant factor in the evolution of a traditional lecture-oriented instructor to a facilitator of classroom collaboration is supportive mentoring from a colleague or a community of supportive faculty. Turning over a measure of control in a classroom where there is so much content to be dealt with can seem very risky. When our efforts meet student resistance, as they almost inevitably do at the start, the active support of colleagues is invaluable. We have found in numerous workshops that it is easy to teach faculty to apply such collaborative techniques as assessment techniques, cognitive maps, and case studies but that the creation of supportive networks among colleagues may be the make-it-or-break-it factor.

References

Blumer, H. *Symbolic Interactionism: Perspective and Method.* Englewood Cliffs, N.J.: Prentice Hall, 1969.

Calkins, L. *The Art of Teaching Writing.* Portsmouth, N.H.: Heinemann, 1986.

Cross, K. P., and Angelo, T. A. *Classroom Assessment Techniques: A Handbook for Faculty.* National Center for Research to Improve Postsecondary Teaching and Learning, 1988.

Ives, E. *The Tape-Recorded Interview: A Manual for Field Workers in Folklore and Oral Histories.* Knoxville: University of Tennessee Press, 1987.

Wigginton, E. *Sometimes a Shining Moment: The Foxfire Experiences.* Garden City, N.Y.: Anchor Books, 1987.

ALLEN EMERSON (Case I) is a doctoral candidate in mathematics education at Western Michigan University.

JERRY PHILLIPS (Case II) is assistant professor of reading at the University of Arkansas, Monticello.

CATHY HUNT (Case III) is professor of microbiology and instructional consultant at Henderson Community College, University of Kentucky.

ARLENE BOWMAN ALEXANDER (Case III) is professor of human services and instructional consultant at Henderson Community College, University of Kentucky.

*This chapter proposes a developmental model for instructors who
wish to establish collaborative learning classrooms.*

Freedom Transformed: Toward a Developmental Model for the Construction of Collaborative Learning Environments

Sharon J. Hamilton

When you reach this final chapter, I wonder whether you feel buffeted by competing views of what constitutes knowledge and knowing in a collaborative learning environment or whether you feel that you have traveled a conceptual path solidly anchored in theoretically consistent soil. My hope is that the path has been sufficiently clear, level, and uniform to enable you to appreciate the potential benefits of collaborative learning in higher education at the individual, institutional, and societal levels. At the same time, the fact that the contributors to this volume have undeniable differences in collaborative learning methods, strategies, tactics, and techniques points to a dramatic range of perspectives on collaborative learning. If we consider that range to be a static representation of the ways in which educators define, articulate, and implement collaborative learning, we really do face competing ideologies and views of what constitutes knowledge and knowing. However, if we consider that range to be a dynamic representation of continual adaptation to different teaching and learning contexts and accommodation to changing student demographics and discipline-specific curricula, we have the basis for a developmental model for the construction of collaborative learning environments. The problem is much more than philosophical or academic. It goes to the heart of the way in which each of us positions himself or herself in relation to the students whom we teach and the subjects that we teach.

Because the preceding chapters have reviewed various areas of the literature on collaborative learning, I will ground my comments primarily in the accumulating lore of collaborative learning—the narrated practices and beliefs of those who have introduced some form of collaborative learning into their classrooms. I use the term *narrated* in a very general sense, because this discussion is based on the stories that I have encountered about collaborative learning practices. I have gathered these stories through a variety of means ranging from informal chats with colleagues at workshops and conferences to formal papers and published articles, including chapters in this volume.

Models of Collaborative Learning

The most obvious characteristic of current practices and beliefs about collaborative learning is diversity. In a considered look at what practitioners and theorists have said, done, and written about collaborative learning over the past several years, John Trimbur (1993) describes the emergence of three distinctive patterns, which he refers to respectively as the *postindustrialist, social constructionist,* and *popular democratic* interpretations of collaborative learning. Although he is still working out descriptions and examples of these models of collaborative learning, I find them helpful when I organize and describe patterns that I have observed over the past decade. These patterns were particularly evident during a recent statewide colloquium on collaborative learning. They can also be seen in this volume despite the concerted attempt of its editors to develop a unified epistemological approach.

The Postindustrialist Model. What Trimbur (1993) calls the postindustrialist model of collaborative learning includes the practices, strategies, and techniques of collaborative learning most amenable to traditional curricula and pedagogy. Closely related to the corporate shift from hierarchically structured decision making to problem solving through group consensus, this model of collaborative learning appears in classrooms in the form of group efforts to solve common problems formulated by an instructor whose curricular agenda determines group structure, time on task, goals, and anticipated answers. Similar to the corporate world, wherein the best proposal wins the bid whether it was developed individually or consensually, groups are often set up to compete with each other to arrive at the most right answers or the best answers. In this view of collaborative learning, pedagogical approaches draw on cognitive-based concepts of teaching, such as mastery learning and effective instruction, in which the individual mastery of curricular content is the ultimate goal of classroom activity. The work of Johnson and Johnson (1991), Slavin (1990), and others related to the cooperative learning movement are representative of this model of collaborative learning. Many educators have heralded this orientation to teaching and learning because it helps to engage students actively in their learning and to develop the social skills of negotiation and idea sharing, while the teacher retains control of all essential decisions about task design, procedures, reporting of results, and follow-up.

The Social Constructionist Model. The goals of engaging students more actively in their learning while concurrently developing social skills of negotiation and consensus building are also part of the second model of collaborative learning that Trimbur (1993) has described, the social constructionist model. However, that is as far as the similarities go. In the social constructionist model of collaborative learning, classrooms of students in a particular discipline are viewed as a common discourse community, a community that will work together to solve common problems through the collective understanding of all, including the instructor. While still very much responsible for curricular decisions as well as for day-to-day classroom management, the instructor in a social constructionist collaborative learning environment shares many decisions about content coverage and learning procedures with students. Together they work at discipline-specific problems, issues, and application of concepts, exploring the course and constructing meaning about the discipline in ways that vary from class to class. The idiosyncratic synergy of each classroom of students leads them to define and design course procedures and course content in different ways. Such a classroom clearly breaks with the postindustrialist model, which still guarantees that the instructor controls the coverage of a particular body of knowledge. In the social constructionist model, first presented as a theoretical framework for collaborative learning by Kenneth Bruffee (1984) and extended more pragmatically for classroom application by Peter Elbow and Pat Belanoff (Elbow and Belanoff, 1989), coverage is less important than the communal process of coming to understand the salient and dynamic ways of thinking and making meaning within a particular discipline. The challenge for instructors is to enable students to build on common and shared interests, motivations, and discipline-specific knowledge while simultaneously capitalizing on idiosyncratic collective knowledge to build bridges to the new body of knowledge and ways of knowing that are particular to a specific course.

The Popular Democratic Model. While the social constructionist model of collaborative learning is predicated on a common investment within a shared discourse community, the third model or pattern of collaborative learning described by Trimbur (1993), the popular democratic model, is predicated on difference. It presents in essence a pedagogical imperative for the multicultural, multilingual, polyglot classroom of the urban university of the twenty-first century. "If the social constructionist model assumes the classroom to be a community of like-minded individuals," says Trimbur, "the popular democratic model assumes each classroom to be a city of strangers." And it is undeniable that, as increasing numbers of nontraditional students flock to our universities, they will indeed see themselves as strangers among strangers. The challenge is for instructors not to obliterate essential differences in the search for commonalities but rather to envision these essential differences—age, race, color, economic status, background, motivation, or prior knowledge—as catalysts for the making of meaning within the specific concepts of the particular course. History, physics, language, mathematics, sociology, psychology, biology—every course of studies enters into our lives throughout our lives in very different ways. Who we are and how we have lived give each of us different orientations to these disciplinary areas so that the very ways of how these subjects come to mean something in our lives is open to examination and discussion. For disciplinary studies, each assumption and convention therefore becomes an aspect to be uncovered and intellectually poked about through the varying perspectives of class members. Traditional notions of coverage and of shared or common background are displaced by multiperspective negotiations about the governing paradigms and tacit traditions of the subject and course and whether they should still govern, remain tacit, and remain traditions. Few examples of this model appear in the literature about collaborative learning; James Berlin's work at Purdue University (Berlin and Vision, 1992), where he and his students together unravel the fabric of course assumptions, values, and conventions, offers the major example I have encountered of current pedagogy situated in the popular democratic approach to teaching and learning.

Considering the Models to Be Continuous and Developmental

As you read the preceding paragraphs, you may have sought to locate your own pedagogical assumptions and practices, as well as ideas that you encountered in the preceding chapters or in workshops, conferences, or other texts, in relation to the models just described. If so, the next question might be, Which of these models or interpretations is appropriate for you and your students, your disciplinary area, and your institutional context? Are they mutually exclusive? That is, is each model based on such completely different assumptions about knowledge and ways of knowing that you could not possibly embrace the practices and beliefs of more than one? Or are they potentially developmental and transitional, representing a continuum of theory and practice that you can anticipate moving along as you work to establish increasingly collaborative, decreasingly teacher-directed learning environments? Noted educational theorists, such as James Britton, Harold Rosen, and John Dixon, all staunch proponents of collaborative learning, in heated debate about cooperative learning at an international conference that I attended on issues in language learning in Ottawa, Canada, in 1986, answered yes to the first question and no to the second. However, when I raised the question during the process of editing this sourcebook, Kris Bosworth, coeditor of this volume, and instructors representing all levels of education spoke of the support that moving through the different models gives a teacher who was new to the ideas and practices of collaborative learning. Thus, with some hesitancy about theoretical eclecticism, I have generated a developmental gloss to lay over the interpretations just described. I offer it here as a tentative model working toward a developmental model. I anticipate that comments from readers will let me know the extent to which it clarifies or confounds their implementation of collaborative learning in their classrooms.

Developing Expertise with Collaborative Learning

The developmental model that I am about to describe draws primarily on the notion of expertise generated by Hubert and Stuart Dreyfus (Dreyfus and Dreyfus, 1986), although I acknowledge that these or similar stages are prevalent throughout the psychological literature on expertise. Michael Carter (1991) has already taken the fives stages articulated by Dreyfus and Dreyfus (1986) beyond the application to artificial intelligence in his discussion of what makes an expert writer. I wish to extend his discussion of stages of expertise in advanced composition to a developmental model of pedagogical expertise that can support educators who wish to establish effective collaborative learning environments. However, my application of the five stages will be less algorithmic and more aleatory than the original model, since my intended use is directed wholly to human interactions, not to a comparison of human and artificial intelligence.

Stage One: Learning Rules, Techniques, and Strategies. With reference to the establishment of collaborative learning environments, educators in this initial stage learn about the various approaches to collaborative learning, the various strategies that can be used to help groups work together, and techniques for planning, managing, and evaluating collaborative learning. Learning is done through reading, conferences, workshops, courses, personal learning experiences, observations, and chats with colleagues, not directly in the classroom with students. Also, the learning involves not so much rules as experience-based, theory-driven approaches, strategies, and techniques. For example, in this volume alone, James Flannery has explored major approaches to collaborative learning; Kris Bosworth has outlined strategies for the development of group skills; Judith Miller, John Trimbur, and John Wilkes have described collaborative learning in a biology class in terms of personality differences; Craig Nelson has discussed techniques for linking collaborative learning and critical thinking; Patricia Sullivan has reviewed strategies particularly applicable to collaborative learning in a computer-based environment; Sharon Cramer has presented several methods for the evaluation of collaborative work; and Jeanne Gerlach has traced a conceptual framework where all the ideas just reviewed intermesh. You have also read several experience-based case studies of successful collaborative learning in classrooms of differing size and discipline. Simply having read and engaged intellectually with this volume or other volumes or having participated in workshops or conferences on collaborative learning puts the reader into this first stage of becoming expert in establishing a collaborative learning environment.

Stage Two: Applying What You Have Learned. The second stage involves applying the approaches, strategies, and techniques that seem most appropriate to particular teaching contexts while learning increasingly sophisticated strategies and techniques. Since you cannot try all the strategies that you have learned or read about at the same time, you are most likely to choose the ones that mesh the most smoothly with your present teaching situation. You will keep the ones that work and drop the ones that are less successful from your repertoire. The danger at this stage is that the most structured and teacher-directed strategies may often be the ones that appear to be the most successful, because they align closely with teachers' and students' expectations of how a classroom should be run and of how knowledge is acquired or developed. These highly structured teacher-directed strategies and techniques, which fit primarily into the postindustrial model that Trimbur (1993) describes, may result in efficient group work but not necessarily in engaged intellectual collaboration. While highly structured strategies provide reinforcement for the classroom efficacy of collaborative learning, early success with such strategies can reduce the motivation or felt need to progress to less predictable, less convergent collaborative techniques that demand more conceptual engagement and divergent intellectual commitment from students. Techniques that move students away from receiving or discovering the knowledge that the teacher has planned for them to learn and toward the negotiating and constructing of understanding on a basis of shared yet disparate conceptions, backgrounds, and experiences are initially more difficult for both students and teachers. When expectations are spelled out in terms of a problem to be solved or a task to be achieved, progress often comes to be defined in terms of product, and the rich process of sharing, give and take, and coming to new understanding powered by group synergy can become lost. Consequently, if the product is no more satisfactory than it is in traditional classes or if it somehow evolves tangentially rather than directly in response to the problem or task, students and teachers alike may consider collaborative work to be an inefficient use of time. Learning how to give students sufficient structure to explore ideas collaboratively without restraining their opportunities to contribute their voices and knowledge to a new and unpredictable construction of understanding takes time and experimentation on the part of students and instructors alike.

Stage Three: Developing Competence. At the third stage, instructors make experience-based decisions about the approaches, strategies, and techniques that are best suited to the achievement of their curricular and pedagogical goals. For example, you may find that the principle of an icebreaking activity during the first class of the semester is good but that the ones you have read about, while advancing your goal of having students get to know each other as soon as possible, do not advance any of your content-specific goals. If time is a critical factor and curricular concerns are of prime importance, you may decide either to eschew the icebreaking activity or to design one yourself that achieves content-specific as well as social goals. For example, in a history class, rather than using a generic icebreaker, you might ask students to identify the historian who has most influenced their thinking, or the historical

event that they consider to have been most catalytic in shaping a particular historical era, or—for a freshman class—their view of what comprises history.
Depending on the size of the class, students can share their views with the
whole class, a small group, or just their neighbor. Moreover, you may discover
that your students have excellent ideas about how to work together and that
they (and you) no longer need highly structured teacher-directed activities. In
this stage, teachers come to rely more on their own teaching experiences and
on their students' suggestions and less on strategies and techniques that other
educators have devised for other students in other classrooms. The possibility
exists to move into a social constructionist model of collaborative learning,
where students and instructors work together to construct meaning within the
concepts of a discipline.

Stage Four: Becoming Proficient. "Going beyond competence is going
beyond rules," writes Michael Carter (1991, p. 63) in his discussion of developing expertise. The fourth stage, proficiency, involves moving away from
reliance on external and generic strategies and techniques and toward developing your own collaborative learning procedures in direct interaction with
the students in your class and the goals and objectives of your course. If you
view your class as a community of like-minded individuals and you view the
acquisition of discipline-specific knowledge as a process of communally constructing meaning within course concepts, paradigms, and traditions, you may
find yourself working within the social constructionist model of collaborative
learning. In this case, the strategies that you (and your students) devise will
involve articulating common goals, common metadiscourse, and common procedures for achieving class goals. If you view your class as a collocation of individuals with differing backgrounds, interests, and intellectual agendas and the
acquisition of discipline-specific knowledge as a process of unpacking and critically analyzing the traditional baggage of disciplinary concepts and assumptions, the strategies that you (and your students) devise may be oriented
toward the popular democratic model of collaborative learning, which is aimed
at questioning and exploring the foundations of course content through the
varied perspectives of your students.

Stage Five: Becoming an Expert. When it works, you are an expert.
Admittedly, this oversimplifies the observation that "experts do what works"
(Carter, 1991, p. 64). "Experts react intuitively to most situations without having to rely on rules or plans; instead, they rely on the familiarity that comes
with experience" (Carter, 1991, p. 64, quoting Dreyfus and Dreyfus, 1986).
Having worked with structured strategies, techniques, and approaches; having adapted them to various situations and various classrooms of students; having made a conscious intellectual decision about the interpretation of
collaborative learning that is appropriate for them, their students, and the institutional teaching context, expert instructors can maneuver with maximum flu-
idity and flexibility to enable their students to become expert at learning
collaboratively.

Freedom Transformed: The Reflective Expert

At this point, we reach the freedom transformed to which my title refers. University instructors have far more freedom than educators at the elementary and secondary levels to determine what they teach and how they teach it. Constrained primarily by class size and program objectives, professors are otherwise free to make curricular and pedagogical decisions. Nevertheless, higher education in America is delivered in one predominant format: the information-transmitting lecture. Inspired by the brilliant lectures of their own professor mentors, shaped by school experiences as recipients and then regurgitators of transmitted information, pressured by promotion and tenure criteria based more on research and scholarly publications than on pedagogical achievement, and faced at freshman and sophomore levels with huge classes, professors have had little reason, time, or potential reward for changing their teaching methods to respond to the changing demographics of university students. However, articles in *The Chronicle of Higher Education* focus on teaching with increasing frequency. Ernest Boyer's (1990) *Scholarship Reconsidered: Priorities of the Professoriate* argues that we must reexamine how we view teaching in the academy, particularly its relationship to our other scholarly endeavors. More than at any other time in the history of higher education, teaching is now receiving the attention and earning the respect that it warrants as a scholarly endeavor. Concurrently, investigators are documenting relationships between the establishment of collaborative learning environments and improved student performance (Hamilton-Wieler, 1992; Hamilton and Hansen, 1992), student retention (Treisman, 1985), increasing disciplinary majors (Treisman, 1985), and the breaking down of cross-cultural and other barriers. College instructors, mindful of the relationships between what is taught and how it is taught; mindful that, as information expands exponentially, individuals need to learn to solve academic, workplace, and societal problems collaboratively; and mindful that knowledge is a dynamic social construct, not a fixed mass, are eschewing the familiar information-transmitting lecture as their primary or sole method of teaching. By developing expertise in the establishment of collaborative learning environments, instructors in higher education are transforming traditional views of university teaching. They are transforming their freedom to teach however they see fit into a theoretically grounded scholarly endeavor that responds directly to the changing demographics and continuously evolving needs of our student population.

References

Berlin, J., and Vision, M. (eds.). *Cultural Studies in the English Classroom*. Portsmouth, N.H.: Boynton/Cook, 1992.

Boyer, E. *Scholarship Reconsidered: Priorities of the Professoriate*. Princeton, N.J.: Carnegie Foundation, 1990.

Bruffee, K. A. "Collaborative Learning and the 'Conversation of Mankind.'" *College English,* 1984, *46,* 635–652.

Carter, M. "What Is 'Advanced' About Advanced Composition?" In K. Adams and J. L. Adams (eds.), *Teaching Advanced Composition: Why and How.* Portsmouth, N.H.: Boynton/Cook, 1991.

Dreyfus, H. L., and Dreyfus, S. E. *Mind over Machine: The Power of Human Intuition and Expertise in the Era of the Computer.* New York: Free Press, 1986.

Elbow, P., and Belanoff, P. *Sharing and Responding.* New York: Random House, 1989.

Hamilton, S. J., and Hansen, E. (eds.). *Sourcebook for Collaborative Learning in the Arts and Sciences.* Bloomington: Center for Media and Teaching Resources, Indiana University, 1992.

Hamilton-Wieler, S. J. *Collaboration: See Treason. Report of a Three-Year Study of Collaborative Learning in Freshman Composition Classrooms.* Bloomington, Ind.: National Council of Teachers of English, 1992. (ED 326900).

Johnson, D. W., and Johnson, R. T. *Learning Together and Alone: Cooperative, Competitive, and Individualistic Learning.* (3rd ed.) Englewood Cliffs, N.J.: Prentice Hall, 1991.

Slavin, R. E. *Cooperative Learning: Theory, Research, and Practice.* Englewood Cliffs, N.J.: Prentice Hall, 1990.

Treisman, P. U. "A Study of the Mathematics Performance of Black Students at the University of California, Berkeley." Unpublished doctoral dissertation, University of California, Berkeley, 1985.

Trimbur, J. "Keynote Address." Address to the Indiana University Colloquium on Collaborative Learning, Indianapolis, March 5, 1993.

SHARON J. HAMILTON (the former Sharon J. Hamilton-Wieler) is associate professor of English in the School of Liberal Arts, Indiana University at Indianapolis.

INDEX

ORDERING INFORMATION

NEW DIRECTIONS FOR TEACHING AND LEARNING is a series of paperback books that presents ideas and techniques for improving college teaching, based both on the practical expertise of seasoned instructors and on the latest research findings of educational and psychological researchers. Books in the series are published quarterly in spring, summer, fall, and winter and are available for purchase by subscription as well as by single copy.

SUBSCRIPTIONS for 1994 cost $47.00 for individuals (a savings of 25 percent over single-copy prices) and $62.00 for institutions, agencies, and libraries. Please do not send institutional checks for personal subscriptions. Standing orders are accepted.

SINGLE COPIES cost $15.95 when payment accompanies order. (California, New Jersey, New York, and Washington, D.C., residents please include appropriate sales tax.) Billed orders will be charged postage and handling.

DISCOUNTS FOR QUANTITY ORDERS are available. Please write to the address below for information.

ALL ORDERS must include either the name of an individual or an official purchase order number. Please submit your order as follows:
    Subscriptions: specify series and year subscription is to begin
    Single copies: include individual title code (such as TL54)

MAIL ALL ORDERS TO:
    Jossey-Bass Publishers
    350 Sansome Street
    San Francisco, CA 94104-1342

FOR SUBSCRIPTION SALES OUTSIDE OF THE UNITED STATES, CONTACT:
    any international subscription agency or Jossey-Bass directly.

OTHER TITLES AVAILABLE IN THE
NEW DIRECTIONS FOR TEACHING AND LEARNING SERIES
Robert J. Menges, Editor-in-Chief
Marilla D. Svinicki, Associate Editor